POSTCARD PHOTOGRAPHERS OF LIVERPOOL AND DISTRICT 1900 = 1939

SEAFORTH, WATERLOO, CROSBY & SEFTON HAMLETS

featuring

S.S.Cushing
B.& A. Feilden
W & Co.
Dove's Library
W.H.Smith
Valentine & Co.
and others

PAUL BOLGER

STATIONS U.K. MERSEYSIDE

The Woods' family outside their 'Seaforth Farm Dairy' at the corner of Thomson and Ewart Roads around 1912 with William presumably tending the pony. The term 'cow-keeper' was a literal one - with refrigeration still largely unpractised, the need for fresh milk required the animals to be stabled locally and this was usually in yards at the rear of the dairies. (Photographer anonymous)

to the memory of
John Roles
whose work in this field was tragically cut short

ACKNOWLEDGEMENTS

Special mention must go to Bob Wright of the Little Crosby Museum,
John Clarkson of Ships In Focus, Tony Cushing and Peter Woolley
whose assistance proved invaluable. Thanks are also due to :-

John Alsop	Ted Gerry	Jim Peden
Bootle Library	Christine Hamer	Dr. Norman H. Reid
John Bourhill	Mrs. R. Hart	Stan Roberts
British Library	Ken Hassell	John Ryan
Gail Collingburn	John B. Horne	St. Andrews University Liby.
Pam Cranston	Gillian Jones	Mark J. Sargant
Crosby Library	Lancashire Record Office	Sea Breezes magazine
Mike Day	Andrew E. Lee-Hart	Ian Simpson
Andrew Douglas	Liverpool Central Libraries	Terry Smith
John Stuart Dove	Liverpool Record Office	W.H.Smith Archive Ltd.
Russell Dove	R. Fraser Mack	Richard Stenlake
Joe Forshaw	Freddy O'Connor	Peter Taylor
Chris Foulds	Ordnance Survey	John Ward

© Paul Bolger
First Published 2005
Stations U.K., P.O. Box 462
Southport, PR8 3WA

Printed in England by The Amadeus Press Ltd.

ISBN 0 947562 08 7

Unless credited otherwise, the illustrations
in this book are from the author's collection.

Having 'Irwin & Sons, Bootle' pencilled on the reverse but with
nothing else to identify the location, this anonymously published
card could be any one of the 12 Bootle branches of this large grocery chain.

CONTENTS

INTRODUCTION

Welcome to the **Bootle, Seaforth, Waterloo, Crosby & Sefton Hamlets** edition of a series of books featuring the pre-war days of the picture postcard - a time when sending one was almost as commonplace as today's telephone call.

In a world of e-mails, faxes, phone texting and the internet, it is easy to forget how the vast majority of our predecessors communicated prior to the I.T. revolution; the humble telephone was as 'high-tech' as things got in that period but few people had one.

If you needed to convey a message in those days you either cycled there, sent a telegram, postcard or in the unlikely event that the other party had a phone, sought out a shop displaying a 'You May Telephone From Here' sign (street kiosks did not become common until 1935) - thus, the postcard was the cheapest and most practical way for the masses to make contact. A card was usually delivered within hours - providing the address was not too distant. There were no fewer than four postal deliveries a day and cards that survive this period often read *'will call upon you this afternoon'* etc. - see page 52 (lower view).

From the 16th June 1897 the Post Office no longer forbade the writing of a message on the address side of a postcard and with the other becoming completely free for an illustration, many publishers decided to enter the market. The introduction of the 'divided back' card in January 1902 formalised matters and hosts of other entrepreneurs joined in. In a relatively short space of time shops offered fine displays of picture postcards and the trend grew so rapidly that 860 million per annum were being posted by 1908. Many people bought them to keep as well as use - this is supported by the large number of surviving cards that were never posted.

The most common subjects were streets, churches, village greens, parks and civic buildings like Town Halls. The fact that so many escaped destruction is not only indicative of the numbers produced, it is great testimony to the skill of the photographers whose task was far from easy. Cameras of the day were substantial and the absence of personal transport confined many to their immediate area.

Established businesses came to dominate the market with photo-mechanical cards and coloured versions - whilst a major part of the industry, these cheaper, mass produced issues are not included in this book. More appealing are the 'real photograph' cards and especially those from the independent studios. Aside from frequently producing higher quality products, their increased local knowledge gave rise to a more adventurous approach and most of the sought after or obscure subjects originate from their cameras - as did many spontaneous and 'one-off' events like disasters and protests. Small they may have been but their combined efforts captured the area's heritage before clearances, developments and bombing re-drew the map.

This book is chiefly concerned with the activities of the local producers of picture postcards in the mid and south Sefton region but some individuals did venture further afield - where this applies, such work will be featured in future volumes. An example being the Feilden brothers - their 'LV' and 'WS' issues refer to series dedicated to Liverpool and Wallasey/Seacombe respectively.

Some had professional High Street studios whilst others were little more than talented amateurs who sold the postcards via stationers shops. The cards travelled widely and it is common to find one sent to the other side of the world - see page 22 lower.

They have also influenced the popularity of local history today - nostalgia features in the press are often triggered by the discovery of an old card.

With the exception of the work undertaken cross-referencing the Valentine collection, an account of this nature could never be complete however many years were devoted to research. In time, it will prove to be 'the tip of the ice-berg' and is, therefore, offered as a springboard for further study as opposed to an infallible record. As the lists imply, thousands of subjects were published but a great many were discarded soon after use. The law of averages dictates that the majority of surviving issues will always favour those from the national publishers with common locations being dominant. On that basis, it is quite possible that a card from an independent producer is now the *sole example* from the lesser number issued. Despite many other hindrances such as anonymous publishers and lack of documentation, it is nonetheless hoped that the following pages give an informative and pleasing insight into the 'golden era' of the picture postcard.

Present day prices are not given as inflation soon renders them out of date but values can also be affected by changing trends and market forces. I am not able to give valuations but for those of you with equally interesting cards, I would welcome the opportunity of purchasing or borrowing same to enhance future volumes. Lists of those in your possession would also help but please ignore coloured or photo-mechanical issues (dot-matrix composition). If you are able to assist, please **do not** send items via the mail; copies or descriptions will always suffice in the first instance. Any help given will be acknowledged and suitably rewarded.

Paul Bolger, 2005.

During early research it became apparent that little was known about many of the independent pre-war postcard photographers. As regards anonymous or fragmented material calculated guesses have had to be made from the few clues that survive. Occasionally, an odd issue surfaces which serves to identify a host of cards - initials not present on the others, a note on the reverse or reference within the correspondence. With the march of time, the origin of many can now only be assumed and especially those that were privately commissioned.

All that can reasonably be done to assemble an overview of this profession has been done but that is all it can ever be. Despite the duration of their activities, if they were amateur and worked from home tracing their name is now almost impossible.

The absence of numbered subjects also makes the size of their portfolios difficult to assess - applying the 1 : 5 ratio in the case of Cushing (see page 6) is not wholly reliable as the numbers produced over 30 years greatly influence the calculation. 1 : 50 is nearer the mark if the period of trading was much smaller - only 2% of the similarly sized 'Parisian Studios' catalogue has been recorded thus far but post-marks suggest they only issued cards for a fraction of that time - between 1905 and 1908 (this company will be featured in later volumes as they rarely ventured north of the Bootle boundary).

Even when descendants can be traced, few can tell you more than is already known. However, periods when the independents were active are easier to determine thanks to post-marks, directories and newspaper archives. Although some cards were postally used up to twenty years after publication, research indicates that the majority were used within a few years of the image being taken - see Bootle Metropole illustration on page 77.

Photographers at High Street premises were kept fairly busy with portraiture and only occasionally, if at all, issued the type of cards subject of this series - a glance opposite will show how most earned a living. With doting parents and the vain prepared to pay 6d. each for small prints, studio work was far more lucrative than 'penny postcards' and explains why many abstained. Despite the professional chauvinism which abounded then, photography was not a male preserve - the artistic opportunities attracted many lady practitioners also.

As regards qualification for inclusion, it is simple - anyone, known or otherwise who issued 'real-photo' postcards of the area's topography and social history between 1900 & 1939. Stationers and Booksellers are also included where known to have commissioned postcards or marked the work of others with their own identity.

The size of this project dictated more than one book and regional volumes were decided upon because most people collect postcards by area. Also, as many publishers confined themselves to a district, it made sense to present the findings accordingly.

To keep duplication to a minimum, compromises have been made but as a general rule, only Sefton subjects appear in this volume. Thus, Cushing's work in other districts is only referred to here and not detailed. Exceptions do apply if the 'foreign' subjects are few in number such as those issued by the already mentioned Parisian Studios - with less than a dozen Sefton postcards being identified from their 2,600 plus portfolio, all known 'P.S.' issues will be included in the Liverpool editions.

All known cards are included and tabulated thus :-
1.   serial number (if applicable).
2.   date or circa (C) or postmark (P) if known.

3.   a description of the subject.
Entries in italics denote the subject is illustrated within the book - refer to the given page.

LISTED PHOTOGRAPHERS 1900 - 1939
(dates approximate with those known or suspected to have issued cards marked #) *PUBLISHING STATIONERS & BOOKSELLERS* are also included and shown in italics.

Edwardian studio poses. (above) A study of an elderly gentleman taken at Hartley Bros. No.2 South Road premises in Waterloo - this establishment was taken over by Arthur W. Partoon in 1912 (see photograph on page 74). (above right) With a smile that would melt any heart, this little lady was immortalised by Charles Cantrell of Bootle. (right) The reverse of this 4" x 2½" view (or 'carte-de-visite' as they were often called) advertises his services in typical style. Note that copies cost sixpence each which was many times the price of a picture postcard. (courtesy of Gillian Jones).

S. S. CUSHING

Stephen Sibbald Cushing of Crosby was one of the most prolific photographers of his day taking thousands of exposures of the area and beyond up to his death on 25th January 1937 at the age of 68. He was the proprietor of a stationery shop at No.4 Moor Lane which first appears in the directory of 1904 - a date that coincides with the earliest known of his published photographs. It seems fitting that a book celebrating his work should follow the 100th anniversary of same.

His early efforts centred on the immediate area but as he progressed he ventured further afield and began numbering the images. Had he not done so, the extent of his labours might not have been fully appreciated as his records have not survived him - however, a rigorous search has identified approximately 20% of his portfolio.

This figure is a calculated guess based upon the ratio of surviving cards in his 1 to 2425 series (see list beginning on page 11). The 'L' & 'T' series support this rule but those prefixed 'M' cannot have totalled the quantity suggested by the numbers (i.e.) up to 1106 - if they had, at least a hundred or more would have survived. With regard to his pre-numbering period, the same equation allows us to assume he took 300 or so prior to No.1. Totting up and making allowances for the known un-numbered items such as commissions and specials, I suspect his grand total of subjects was beyond the 3000 mark. With further scrutiny, it is reasonable to assume that 'L' stood for Litherland but what the other pre-fixes signified is a mystery. Given his known arrangements with sub-post offices like Richardson of Fazakerley (more of which later), I imagine 'M' & 'T' stood for the initials of other, as yet untraced, individuals or outlets.

As business expanded he opened a second shop in School Lane, Formby. Seed's Southport directories and the addition of Formby subjects suggest this was around 1906 - it is not listed after 1909 and therefore reasonable to assume it proved less remunerative and was closed.

 Stephen S. Cushing and his camera pictured at the rear of his Crosby shop around 1930. (courtesy Tony Cushing)

At this point it should be noted that coloured postcards exist of Formby subjects with the backs indicating they were published by 'Cushing's Library, Formby'. Although outside the parameters of this study, nothing else is known of this venture and it must be assumed, therefore, that they too proved unsuccessful.

By sub-letting part of a post-office he also had a third outlet in the Fazakerley district and almost certainly another in Tuebrook but more of those and the related subjects in the next volume - Liverpool North.

His ability behind the lens led to him being retained as Crosby Borough photographer and examples of such work can be seen on later pages. Whilst he sold his postcards in his own outlets, he also retailed them through other businesses. Evidence of this exists in the form of one card taken in 1905 marked 'Newcombe', 89 St. Johns Road, Waterloo, on the reverse. Towards the end of his days Cushing entered into another joint venture with the 'One-Day Photo Service' of 31 Alexandra Road, Crosby who continued to manage things after his death.

What cannot be determined accurately is how long Cushing's material was published beyond 1937. As no post-marks later than 1940 have been noted, it is probable the collection was little used afterwards. Even if some post-war demand had existed, the majority of the images would certainly have appeared dated by then. With interest in matters historical not being what they are today, it is likely the material was moth-balled by 1950. This is supported by a grand-son who remembers glass negatives stored in the loft of his home around that time - also that what remained were consigned to the tip some time in the 1960's. Had they remained in store a decade or so longer, the local history boom could have been their saviour.

As his coverage of the Crosby district reached saturation point, why he didn't exploit Bootle and other districts of Liverpool more vigorously is curious when considering the opportunities within easy reach - they were no more distant than areas he already visited. Judging by the photos un-earthed to date, Cushing seems to have had a preference for the picturesque - there were fewer leafy lanes amid Liverpool and Bootle's industry and high-density housing. Other reasons may have been his obligations to the borough or that he had simply reached full capacity; dark-room work was far more time consuming then with heavy fibre-based papers requiring lengthier processes.

As will be seen from the examples on the following pages, Stephen Cushing's cards can be identified in a number of ways. His early work was un-numbered but many captions bear a distinctive slant with due accent on certain letters such as 'R' and 'A'. When numbering was first introduced, he encircled them with a 'C' but this practice soon died out. Cruder styles of captioning were also employed - both before

numbering and beyond the 2000 milestone. So unlike his 'copperplate' style, they suggest that others were involved and particularly for the 'M' issues. Regular, sepia, bordered and borderless cards have all been noted but borderless & sepia are generally earlier with bordered & regular cards dominating the latter decades. Some 1920's scenes include a large dog - this was the family pet, Prince, who often accompanied him.

As with other photographers, he is known to have diverted from normal practice more than once to capture the unusual (see page 20) - although appearing to be the work of another,

the backs clearly name Stephen Cushing as the cameraman. In the latter third of his crusade, the backs of cards were routinely stamped with his name and usually in green ink - either 'Stephen S. Cushing - Photographer' or 'S.S.Cushing - Gt.Crosby' for example. The trademark 'Crosloo Series' also appears during this period.

Judging by his known Sefton subjects (from page 11), he probably took at least one photo of the borough's streets prior to 1936. So, if you haven't found yours, keep searching - it almost certainly exists thanks to the wonderful legacy left by Stephen S. Cushing.

(left) A full frontal view of the Crosby shop around 1910 and definitive enough to allow a detailed inspection of the goods on show. The left hand window has stationery and all manner of fancy goods and gifts including ornaments and fire-screens. Note also, the tall column of picture postcards just to the left of the door - all from Stephen Cushing's camera, no doubt. The month this photo was taken would appear to have been December for two reasons - the offer of private Christmas cards at 2/- per dozen and the 40º F (5º C) registering on the 'Stephen's Inks' thermometer. The right hand display concentrates on toys with clockwork trains, games, boxes of lead figures, dolls-house furniture and animals much in evidence. Both windows have rows of books at the bottom and these most likely form part of the 'circulating library' stock - a service that many shops once offered. (courtesy of Tony Cushing) (right) The Coronation Road shopping arcade (opposite Harrington Road) around 1912 showing the cast-iron and glass awnings which once sheltered the public and avoided the need for canvas shop-blinds. The shoe repairers on the right are 'Coombe's' with prices from 10d. to 3/6d - the latter being for 'Gents Boots Soled and Heeled'. Premises beyond (right to left) include Harris' shoeshop, Passmore's drapery, Dawber's newsagents, Duckles' grocers & Halliwell's confectioners.

 (bottom) Coronation Rd from Islington around 1930. Banner's stonemasons and the council schools are on the right whilst opposite is Livock & Edwards' garage and petrol station - although abandoning fuel sales in the mid-90's, this garage was still trading under the same name until closure in 2004.

CORONATION ROAD GREAT CROSBY

T54

2222. CORONATION ROAD GT CROSBY

 (Opposite) Crosby village when Stephen Cushing was in his prime. The number of pubs will surprise many with long forgotten ones being the *Crosby Vaults* (opposite the Police Station) the *Ship Hotel* (opposite the George Hotel) the *Islington Hotel* (corner of Vale Road) and the *Boar's Head* (junction of Victoria Road and Cook's Lane). The latter was demolished not long afterwards when Cook's Lane was widened and renamed Manor Road. Many parts are still recognisable and note the amount of greenbelt still in place. As with most areas that have seen redevelopment, the all conquering motor car is mainly responsible for the changes since then - a bypass, two large car-parks and the inevitable supermarket. Also worthy of mention is the 'Great Crosby Machine Brick Works Ltd.' on Cook's Lane (now Manor Road) and the still largely residential nature of Moor Lane.

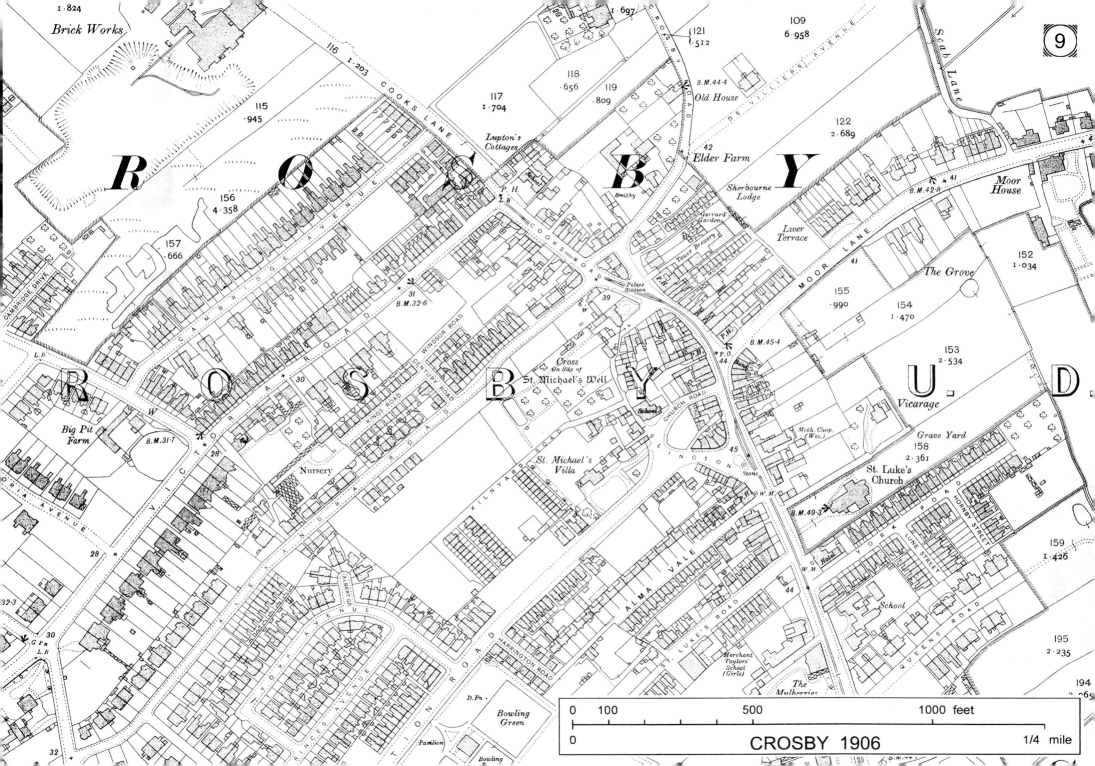

CROSBY 1906

THE BOULDER STONE GREAT CROSBY

(left) One of the most photographed sites in the Sefton area was the 20 ton Boulder Stone in Crosby village and this Cushing view of it dates from about 1905. Also referred to as the 'Gypsum Boulder', it is said to have been an Ice Age glacial deposit from Cumberland and was un-earthed in Cooks Lane (later Manor Road) in 1898. As we see here, this significant geological find was mounted at the junction of Islington and Liverpool Road but removed in 1926 to the Coronation Road Recreation Ground where it remains today. Behind the elderly gentleman are two of Islington's original shops namely James Guy's butchers (No.11) and Sam Yick's laundry (No. 13). These were demolished in 1935 with the rest of the block which included cottages, a public weighing machine and the 'Islington Hotel' pub at the corner of Vale Road.

(right) With at least five examples (including another on Page 12), 'Bird's eye views' were popular subjects for Stephen Cushing and this version of Formby from his un-numbered period automatically dates it around 1904. Looking north-west from the top of the Royal Hotel on Liverpool Road, the junction with Raven Meols Lane can be seen to the right of the large detached building pictured left of centre. Although this survives today, many of the properties in the immediate area have been lost to redevelopment. Although the caption doesn't have Cushing's usual flourish, the back of the card is identical to those known to have been issued by him - occasional caption variations such as this can make some cards difficult to identify.

BIRDS EYE VIEW OF FORMBY

CUSHING S S

No.	Date	Location or Subject
~		AGNES ROAD, BLUNDELLSANDS
~		ALBERT COTTAGE, OXFORD ROAD, WATERLOO
~		ALEXANDRA PARK, GREAT CROSBY
~		*BIRDS EYE VIEW OF FORMBY - see illustration opposite*
~	*1919 P*	*BOULDER STONE, GREAT CROSBY - see illus. opposite.*
~	1907	BURST CANAL AT FORD - APRIL 14TH 1907
~	1904 P	CAMBRIDGE ROAD ('Compliments of Season')
~		CHAPEL LANE, FORMBY
~		COLLEGE ROAD, CROSBY (north from Marine F.C.)
~		COOKS ROAD TOWARDS CROSBY POLICE STATION
~		COOKS ROAD TOWARDS VICTORIA ROAD
~	1929	CROSBY CARNIVAL (6)
~		CROSBY? FIRE ENGINE & STAFF
~	1904 P	CROSBY HALL, INCE BLUNDELL
~		*CROSBY RD & SOUTH RD SHELTER - see ill. page 22.*
~		ELM TREE COTTAGE, CROSBY HALL
~		GARDEN OF REMEMBRANCE, GREAT CROSBY
~	1913 P	GRANGE LANE, FRESHFIELD
~		*GREAT CROSBY DUST-CART - see illustration page 20.*
~		HAIGH ROAD, WATERLOO
~	1905	HALL ROAD DISASTER (sold by 'Newcombe')
~		HALSALL LANE, FORMBY (Cushing's shop)
~	1907 P	'HOLYROOD' BLUNDELLSANDS (House)
~		INCE BLUNDELL HALL
~	1915 P	THE LAKE, INCE BLUNDELL
~		LITTLE CROSBY CHURCH
~	1913 P	LIVERPOOL ROAD, GREAT CROSBY (Moor Lane)
~		LIVERPOOL ROAD & THE GREEN, GREAT CROSBY
~		*LIVERPOOL RD & LANGAN'S PLACE - see illus. page 28.*
~		LIVERPOOL ROAD & LITTLE CROSBY ROAD
~	1902	SS 'MATADOR' ON BLUNDELLSANDS SHORE
~	*1912*	*MOOR LANE, GREAT CROSBY - see illustration page 28.*
~	1930 C	NAZARETH HOUSE, GREAT CROSBY (group pose)
~		PIGEON LOFT 'SEASONS GREETINGS' (Vale Road?)
~		THE POOL, INCE WOODS
~	1921	PRINCE OF WALES @ GT.CROSBY 5/7/21 - Uncircled
~	*1921*	*(as above) - Circled 2 - see illustration page 20.*
~	1921	WAITING FOR PRINCE/WALES @ CROSBY - Circled 3
~	1921	'HERE HE COMES' PR/WALES @ CROSBY - Circled 4
~	1908 P	THE RECTORY, SEFTON
~		RIVERSLEA (House)
~	1933	ST.HELENS CHURCH, GREAT CROSBY
~	1911 P	THE SERPENTINE, BLUNDELLSANDS
~		SOUTH ROAD, WATERLOO (with Xmas greeting)
~		THORPES ROAD & ISLINGTON
~		VICARAGE AVENUE, GREAT CROSBY
~	1912 P	VICTORIA ROAD, FRESHFIELD
~		WARRENHOUSE ROAD, BLUNDELLSANDS
~	1905 P	WESLEYAN CHURCH, BLUNDELLSANDS (portrait)
~	1905 P	W.L.L. GOLF CLUB, BLUNDELLSANDS
1		INCE BLUNDELL HALL
2	1908 P	LION LODGE, INCE BLUNDELL
4	1905 P	THE LAKE, INCE BLUNDELL
7	1940 P	INCE BLUNDELL HALL
8		INCE BLUNDELL CHAPEL (interior)
9	1908 P	LODGE GATES, INCE BLUNDELL
10	1909 P	ROAD TO INCE WOODS
11		CROSBY HALL WEST LODGE, INCE BLUNDELL
13		WISHING WELL, SEFTON
14		CROSBY ROAD, WATERLOO
17		CROSBY HALL
18	1907 P	INCE WOODS, INCE BLUNDELL (roundhouse)
19		CROSBY HALL
2X		BLUNDELLSANDS ROAD - BY AGNES ROAD
22		GREAT STONE, CROSBY VILLAGE
24		LITTLE CROSBY
25	1906 P	INCE WOODS
27	1910 P	ST.LUKES CHURCH, CROSBY
31		NICHOLAS ROAD, BLUNDELLSANDS
32	1911 P	INCE WOODS
38	1905 P	SEFTON CHURCH
44		STOCKS, THORNTON
47	1907 P	ST.LUKES, GREAT CROSBY (interior)
55		INCE WOODS
58		CROSBY & BLUNDELLSANDS STATION
63		INCE WOODS
66	1911 P	INCE BLUNDELL VILLAGE
68		SQUIRE BLUNDELL, CROSBY HALL (& dogs)
70	1907 P	SQUIRE BLUNDELL, CROSBY HALL (pony & trap)
78	1907 P	BOSWELL STREET, BOOTLE
81		HALL ROAD STATION
90		MARINE TERRACE
97	1905 P	CROSBY, BLUNDELLSANDS STATION (& Train)
100	1906 P	DERWENT ROAD, CROSBY
106		INCE WOODS
119		THATCHED COTTAGES, COOKS RD (card '0119')
128		BLUNDELLSANDS HOTEL
133	1905 P	CROSBY HALL
134		ST.MARY'S, LITTLE CROSBY
135		LITTLE CROSBY
136	1918 P	LITTLE CROSBY
137		ST.MARYS, LITTLE CROSBY (interior)
138		OXFORD ROAD, WATERLOO
144		INCE WOODS
146		LIVERPOOL ROAD SHOPS OPP. ISLINGTON, CROSBY
148		INCE WOODS

BIRDS EYE VIEW GREAT CROSBY.

361

(below) The first 'Grapes Hotel' in Thornton as photographed by Stephen Cushing around 1905 and given the number 359. As can be seen on the opposite page, he then focused upon the nearby 'Nags Head' (which became 360) before returning to the village and taking a 'Birds eye view of Great Crosby' (No. 361 pictured left). Encircling that number with a 'C' but not No. 359 indicates he was tiring of his customary trademark by then.

(above) This view looking due east from the top of the Tower Brewery in Crosby village was almost certainly taken in 1905 as the listing opposite would suggest. The rear of the Liver Terrace houses on Moor Lane are bottom right and the block beyond consisted of four larger terraced properties which included Mrs. Jane Graham's private school - note the flagpole of same protruding through the trees at the rear. Scab Lane is hidden from view behind those trees and note the rows of harvested wheat in the large expanse of farmland further on - the Crosby Windmill can also be seen in the middle distance. (courtesy of Crosby Library - reference win/gc 32)

GRAPES HOTEL

359.

THORNTON N9 LIVERPOOL

(right) Stephen Cushing visited Hightown on at least three occasions according to the reference numbers of cards discovered to date, the first of which appears to have been around 1912 when he exposed a minimum of seven plates. He may have taken more on that visit but there was little to point a camera at in those early days of the settlement - a few lanes, a handful of businesses, a station, pub and village green. Here is one of that clutch featuring the latter with shops to the left and the original bank, a tiny wooden hut, visible on the extreme right. For some unknown reason, he saw fit to include his name on the front of the Hightown cards - apart from isolated examples, this wasn't something he did generally (Cushing No.1808).

 (left) With a reference number that has mislead many, this Cushing view of Crosby Road South towards the Overhead Railway's station at Seaforth Sands was taken early in 1922 and not 1950. This was journey's end for tramway travellers from Crosby and the tall open-sided car shed can be seen beyond the right of the tram. The large building to the right of that is the railway's original terminus of 1894 which was converted to a carriage shed in 1925. The posters beneath the staircase promote Bird's custard, Horniman's tea, Windsor toffee and HP sauce - a 'Rotunda' theatre billboard can also be seen.

Note that ten years separate the postcards on this page yet the reference numbers are only 142 apart - the first world war and austere post-war conditions no doubt accounting for Cushing's inactivity during this period.

1468	1907 P	*ALT COTTAGE, HALL ROAD - see illustration page 71.*
1516	1908 P	ALTCAR CHURCH
1606		BLUNDELLSANDS SHORE & BEACHED ROWING BOAT
1608	1908 P	FORMBY SHORE (looking towards Altcar)
1639	1911 P	*GRAPES HOTEL, FRESHFIELD - see illustration page 26.*
1661		LITTLE CROSBY WAR MEMORIAL
17XX	1916 P	ST.MICHAELS CHURCH (corrugated)
1738	1906 P	CROSBY MILL
1739		SQUIRE, CROSBY HALL (& car) WM.JOS.BLUNDELL
1746		WRIGHT'S PIT, GREAT CROSBY
1747	1916 P	MANOR ROAD
1748		COOKS ROAD, CROSBY
1750		MOOR LANE, CROSBY (to village)
1752		VICARAGE AVENUE, GREAT CROSBY
1753		ST.LUKE'S CHURCH
1757	1911 P	CROSBY MILL (portrait)
1760	1910 P	THE DELPH, LITTLE CROSBY
1762		BLUNDELLSANDS SHORE
1763	1916 P	MILL & MOOR LANE, CROSBY
1776		ST.PETER & ST.PAULS CHURCH, GREAT CROSBY
1777	1911 P	SEAFIELD CONVENT, GREAT CROSBY
1778		ST.MICHAEL'S CROSS & WELL
1781		CAMBRIDGE AVENUE, GREAT CROSBY
1784		CAMBRIDGE AVENUE, GREAT CROSBY
1785	1916 P	COOKS ROAD, CROSBY VILLAGE
1791	1921 P	GYPSUM BOULDER, CROSBY
1792	1911 P	ALEXANDRA PARK, CROSBY
1795	1910 C	POPLAR AVENUE, GREAT CROSBY
1796		ESHE ROAD
1798		WESLEYAN CHAPEL, BLUNDELLSANDS
1800	1918 P	BLUNDELLSANDS SHORE (New Brighton Tower)
1801		WEST LANCS GOLF CLUB, BLUNDELLSANDS
1803	1915 P	BLUNDELL AVENUE, HIGHTOWN
1807		*RIVER ALT, HIGHTOWN - see illustration page 29*
1808		*THE GREEN, HIGHTOWN - see illustration opposite.*
1810		HIGHTOWN HOTEL
1814		ALT ROAD, HIGHTOWN
1825		THATCHED COTTAGE, MOOR LANE
1830	1918 P	BLUNDELLSANDS SHORE (shrimpers)
1832		LIVERPOOL ROAD, GREAT CROSBY
1834		BLUNDELLSANDS ROAD WEST (to river)
1835	1913 P	FOUNTAIN, BLUNDELLSANDS
1839	1918 P	BLUNDELLSANDS STATION (& LYR Electric)
1840	1926 P	SCHOOL LANE, INCE BLUNDELL
1841	1918 P	BLUNDELLSANDS STATION
1844		CROSBY MILL
1847	1918 P	COOKS ROAD & POLICE STATION, CROSBY
1849		LOWER ALT ROAD, HIGHTOWN
1857	1925 P	CROSBY MILL (with blades - portrait view)
1867		MOOR LANE, CROSBY
1868	1920 C	CORONA CINEMA, COLLEGE ROAD (not yet open)
1869		PRINCES AVENUE, GREAT CROSBY
1870		PRINCES AVENUE, GREAT CROSBY
1875	1920 P	CORONATION ROAD (towards College Road)
1876	6-1920	'SOUTHESK', 'BUENA VISTA' & 'NETHERWOOD'
1877	6-1920	'SOUTHESK' & COAST EROSION, BLUNDELLSANDS
1878	6-1920	*'SOUTHESK' & COAST EROSION - see illus. page 29.*
1879	6-1920	'NETHERWOOD', 'BEACHSIDE TOWERS' & EROSION
1880		BLUNDELLSANDS SHORE
1882		IVY COTTAGE, INCE WOODS
1883		CORONATION DRIVE, GREAT CROSBY
1885	1920 P	KIMBERLEY DRIVE, GREAT CROSBY
1888		KIMBERLEY DRIVE, GREAT CROSBY
1889	1920 P	ST.PETER & PAUL CHURCH
1890		CHURCH OF ST.PETER & ST.PAUL (interior)
1891		CHURCH OF ST.PETER & ST.PAUL (altar)
1900		REGENT CINEMA, CROSBY
1903	1923 P	VICTORIA PARK, WATERLOO
1905	1922 P	QUEENS ROAD
1906	1922 P	COLLEGE AVENUE
1909		ALEXANDRA ROAD, GREAT CROSBY
1910		ST.MARY'S CHURCH, LITTLE CROSBY
1911		ST.MARY'S CHURCH, LITTLE CROSBY
1913	1922 C	LMS RAILWAY, BLUNDELLSANDS (station beyond)
1914		ALEXANDRA ROAD, GREAT CROSBY (to Cooks Road)
1915		ALEXANDRA ROAD, GREAT CROSBY
1929		CROSBY CARNIVAL (12)
1941		BRIDGE ROAD, LITHERLAND
1943	1922 P	*SEAFORTH ROAD, SEAFORTH - see illustration page 24.*
1950		*CROSBY ROAD SOUTH (Seaforth Stn) - see illus. opposite*
1954		STANLEY PARK, LITHERLAND
1955		WAR MEMORIAL, WATERLOO
1958		KELVINSIDE, GREAT CROSBY
1962		ROSEDALE AVENUE, GREAT CROSBY
1963	1922 P	CORONATION ROAD, COUNCIL SCHOOLS
1965	5-1922	HALL ROAD LANDMARK, BLUNDELLSANDS
1966	5-1922	HALL ROAD LANDMARK, BLUNDELLSANDS
1977	1925 P	BLUNDELLSANDS ROAD WEST
1978		VICTORIA ROAD
1979	1922 P	VICTORIA ROAD (to Cooks Road)
1980		VICTORIA ROAD
1983	5-1923	HALL ROAD SHORE, BLUNDELLSANDS
1984		CORONATION ROAD, GREAT CROSBY
1986		YORK AVENUE
1987	1923 P	PROMENADE, BLUNDELLSANDS
1993		SEFTON ROAD, LITHERLAND (to Litherland Park)
1997		ALEXANDRA MOUNT, LITHERLAND
1999		CROSBY MILL
2000		ELTON AVENUE, BLUNDELLSANDS
2001		SHERWOOD ROAD

LITTLE CROSBY RD GT CROSBY 2118

A Waterloo & Crosby Motor Services bus for Seaforth Sands at the junction of Little Crosby Road and Liverpool Road circa 1926 - the service commenced here and replaced the Overhead Railway tram connection which ended in December 1925. The original Crosby police station is just off-camera to the left as the shadow indicates and beyond is the office of Thomas Mawdsley, coal merchant, at No.11 Little Crosby Road. On the right, a signwriter gives a new identity to the old 'Crosby Vaults' pub at Nos. 1 & 3 Liverpool Road - it became Myerscough's Cafe around this time or 'Dining Rooms & Supper Bar' as the sign eventually read (Cushing No.2118)

(Inset & opposite) Items recording the co-ordination of the Crosby bus service and Overhead Railway. Part of an LOR & WCMS handbill from May 1926 and a LOR & Ribble 'through' ticket - the latter succeeding the WCMS in January 1931.

THE LIVERPOOL OVERHEAD RAILWAY

— AND —

WATERLOO AND CROSBY MOTOR SERVICES, LTD.

CHEAP THROUGH RETURN TICKETS

ISSUED ALL DAY

	1st CLASS Return	3rd CLASS Return
Great Crosby to Pier Head, James St. or Custom House -	9d.	7d.
Waterloo [St. John's Road] to Pier Head, James St. or Custom House - (By BUS and OVERHEAD RAILWAY)	8d.	6d.
Seaforth Sands to Pier Head or James St. -	6d.	4d.

2002		MANOR ROAD
2003		CAMBRIDGE ROAD
2004		MANOR AVENUE
2005		CAMBRIDGE AVENUE, GREAT CROSBY
2006	1925 P	CAMBRIDGE AVENUE, GREAT CROSBY
2008		CAMBRIDGE AVENUE, GT. CROSBY (to Cambridge Road)
2010	1925 P	DOWHILLS ROAD
2011		ROSSETT ROAD
2013	1925 P	BLUNDELLSANDS ROAD EAST
2016		CAVENDISH ROAD, BLUNDELLSANDS (to railway)
2022	10-1923	'HOLMSIDE' & COAST EROSION - see illust. page 29.
2024	1925 P	LIVERPOOL ROAD (from Cooks Road)
2028	1925 P	ASHBOURNE AVENUE (boy with dog)
2029		ALEXANDRA PARK, GREAT CROSBY
2030	1926 P	ALEXANDRA PARK, GREAT CROSBY
2036		ST. ANTHONY'S ROAD
2039	1924 C	MOOR LANE, GREAT CROSBY (east to Scape Lane)
2041		MOOR LANE, GREAT CROSBY (to Liverpool Road)
2042		MOOR LANE, GREAT CROSBY
2044		ST. LUKES CHURCH (interior)
2045		ST. LUKES CHURCH (interior)
2047	1925 P	MERSEY ROAD
2050	1925 P	REGINA AVENUE, WATERLOO
2051		WORCESTER AVENUE, WATERLOO
2059		MOUNT PLEASANT, WATERLOO (near King Street)
2073	1925 P	MARINERS ROAD (to Bridge Road)
2074	1925 P	ESHE ROAD
2076		WARREN ROAD
2077	1925 P	BLUNDELLSANDS SHORE (amongst dunes)
2079	1933 P	BLUNDELLSANDS ROAD WEST
2080	1928 P	WARREN ROAD
2081	1928 P	BLUNDELLSANDS ROAD WEST (towards shore)
2083	1928 P	AGNES ROAD (from railway station)
2084		BLUNDELLSANDS ROAD WEST
2085	1928 P	BLUNDELLSANDS ROAD WEST (from Agnes Road)
2087		CORONATION DRIVE, GREAT CROSBY
2089		ALDER GROVE, WATERLOO (to Brooke Road)
2090		ROSSETT ROAD, BLUNDELLSANDS
2092		CEDAR GROVE, WATERLOO
2093		PARK VIEW, WATERLOO
2098		REGINA AVENUE, WATERLOO
2100		BROOKE ROAD, WATERLOO
2104		PINE GROVE, WATERLOO
2105		MYRTLE GROVE, WATERLOO
2110	1928 P	CANAL BRIDGE, LITHERLAND (from Bridge Road)
2112		SEFTON ROAD, LITHERLAND
2113		SEFTON ROAD, LITHERLAND
2115		SEFTON ROAD, LITHERLAND
2118	1928 P	LITTLE CROSBY ROAD (WCMS bus) - see illus. opposite.
2120	1928 P	COAST EROSION, BLUNDELLSANDS
2121		COAST EROSION, BLUNDELLSANDS
2127		COUNCIL GROUNDS, LITHERLAND
2139		MILLER AVENUE
2140		MILLER AVENUE
2141		GYPSUM BOULDER, GREAT CROSBY (in park)
2146	1928 P	BRIDGE RD, BRIGHTON LE SANDS (from Riverslea Rd.)
2147		HARLECH ROAD, BLUNDELLSANDS
2149	1928 P	ALEXANDRA ROAD
2150	1928 P	LIVERPOOL ROAD (from Moor Lane junction)
2166	1928 P	ST. NICHOLAS CHURCH
2167	1927 P	SEAVIEW TERRACE, WATERLOO
2169		SERPENTINE, BLUNDELLSANDS
2171		BLUNDELLSANDS HOTEL (portrait format)
2172		BLUNDELLSANDS HOTEL
2173		TOWN HALL & CARNEGIE LIBRARY, COLLEGE ROAD
2175		ALEXANDRA PARK GARDEN OF REMEMBRANCE
2176		BLUNDELLSANDS SHORE
2178	1929 P	MERSEY ROAD (from College Road)
2179	1929 P	BLUNDELLSANDS SHORE (female bathers)
2183	1929 P	LIVERPOOL ROAD (from Kimberley Road - WCMS bus)
2184		ALEXANDRA PARK, GREAT CROSBY
2185		ALEXANDRA PARK, GREAT CROSBY
2186	1929 P	LIVERPOOL ROAD (from Myers Road - WCMS Bus)
2187	1927 C	LIVERPOOL ROAD & VILLAGE (from Islington)
2188	1927	BLUNDELLSANDS COAST EROSION
2190		WEST LANCS GOLF CLUB
2191	1929 P	LIVERPOOL ROAD (from Cooks Road)
2192	1929 P	ILFORD AVENUE
2193		INCE AVENUE, GREAT CROSBY

CANAL BRIDGE LITHERLAND 2396

(left & below) Both of these Cushing views can safely be regarded as 1932 issues thanks to films released that year. Below, 'The Mummy' starring Boris Karlof is showing at the Corona cinema on College Road, Crosby, whilst a poster displayed near Litherland's canal bridge for the Palladium cinema promotes 'She Wanted a Millionaire' & 'The Frightened Lady' - the numbers on the cards indicating they were taken around the same time. Other visible features of the left-hand view include a Leeds & Liverpool Canal bye-laws poster together with a notice warning vehicles to proceed 'DEAD SLOW'. This swing bridge, built in 1888, was replaced by a wider and stronger lifting one in 1933 (see page 32). The 'Red Lion' can be seen beyond as can the mock-tudor upper storeys of Bridge Road.

The 'Corona' view was taken from the junction of Mersey and College Roads and shows one of Irwin's grocery shops on that corner. The window displays of such establishments were sumptuous compared to today's and the skill of a 'window-dresser' was both a recognised and fairly common occupation - see page 2 also.

COLLEGE ROAD, GREAT CROSBY. 2407

2195	1929 P	MOOR LANE, CROSBY (south to Northern Road)
2197		RAILWAY & STATION. WATERLOO (from Five Lamps)
2206		LINACRE ROAD / BRIDGE ROAD
2208		ST.MARYS CHURCH, GREAT CROSBY
2214	1930 P	INCE AVENUE
2215		DEVILLIERS AVENUE, GREAT CROSBY
2216		DEVILLIERS AVENUE, GREAT CROSBY
2217		WAR MEMORIAL, WATERLOO (portrait)
2222	1930 P	CORONATION RD FROM CROWN BLDGS (elevated)
2223	1930 P	CAMBRIDGE ROAD, GREAT CROSBY
2224		CAMBRIDGE ROAD (to St.Michaels Road)
2225		CAMBRIDGE ROAD, GREAT CROSBY
2226		CAMBRIDGE ROAD, GREAT CROSBY
2230		SHORE, BLUNDELLSANDS
2233		KINGSWAY, CROSBY (near Stuart Road)
2234	1930 P	KINGSWAY, CROSBY (to Stuart Road)
2237		BROWNMOOR LANE, CROSBY
2238	1930 P	BROWNMOOR LANE, CROSBY (older houses)
2239	1930 P	MORNINGSIDE
2240	1930 P	ENDBUTT LANE (& 'Endbutt' pub)
2243		STUART ROAD (near Myers Road)
2244	1930 P	STUART ROAD
2249	1930 P	MOOR LANE
2251		SEAFIELD AVENUE, CROSBY
2254		ROSEDALE AVENUE, GREAT CROSBY
2257		ENFIELD AVE, GREAT CROSBY (to Northern Road)
2258		EVEREST ROAD
2259	1930 P	DEVILLIERS AVENUE
2280	1930 P	BRIDGE RD, BRIGHTON LE SANDS (from Mariners Road)
2282		COAST EROSION
2283		HALL ROAD SHORE (with boy & dog)
2284	1930 P	THE SERPENTINE
2289	1930 P	BROWNMOOR LANE
2292	1930 P	MYERS ROAD
2294	1930 P	KELVINSIDE
2296		BAND STAND, RECREATION GROUND, GT.CROSBY
2297		MERCHANT TAYLORS GIRLS SCHOOL, GT.CROSBY
2298		MERCHANT TAYLORS GIRLS SCHOOL, GT.CROSBY
2301		STANLEY PARK, LITHERLAND
2302		STANLEY PARK, LITHERLAND
2304		HATTON HILL ROAD, LITHERLAND
2305	1932 P	BLUNDELLSANDS COAST EROSION (high tide)
2306	1932 P	BLUNDELLSANDS SHORE (children paddling)
2307		ST.NICHOLAS FOUNTAIN, THE SERPENTINE (portrait)
2308	1932 P	BLUNDELLSANDS SHORE (mother & pram)
2312	1932 P	MERSEY VIEW (from Holden Street)
2313		NICHOLAS ROAD, BLUNDELLSANDS
2321		BLUNDELL ROAD, HIGHTOWN
2324		ILFORD AVENUE
2325		ILFORD AVENUE (to Little Crosby Road)

2327	1932 P	RAWSON ROAD, SEAFORTH
2329	1932 P	SEAFORTH ROAD, SEAFORTH (LMS station visible)
2330	1932 P	SEAFORTH ROAD, SEAFORTH (from Elm Road)
2332	1932 P	COAST ERROSION (high tide - road cordonned)
2334		ST.HELENS CHURCH
2335		ST.HELENS CHURCH (interior)
2336		ST.HELENS CHURCH (interior)
2338	1932 P	SANDY ROAD, SEAFORTH (from Seaforth Road)
2342		HEREFORD ROAD, SEAFORTH (to Rawson Road)
2345	1930	COOKS ROAD - PINFOLD COTTAGE (August 1930)
2346	1930	CROSBY COTTAGE (August 1930)
2348		ST.MICHAELS CHURCH, B/SANDS (altar close up)
2349		ST.MICHAELS CHURCH, BLUNDELLSANDS
2350		ST.MICHAELS CHURCH, BLUNDELLSANDS (interior)
2351		ST.MICHAELS CHURCH, BLUNDELLSANDS (interior)
2352		ST.MICHAELS CHURCH, BLUNDELLSANDS (altar)
2354	1932 P	RECREATION GROUND (boating lake)
2356	1932 P	RECREATION GROUND (slide & children)
2361	1932 P	THE GEORGE HOTEL - MOOR LANE / LPOOL RD
2362	1932 P	RECREATION GROUND (boating lake - overall)
2373		MARINE GARDENS
2376	1934 P	BROWNMOOR PARK
2378		RUTHERGLEN AVENUE, GREAT CROSBY
2379		CRANMORE AVENUE (from Stuart Road)
2383	1934 P	CRANMORE AVENUE
2385		ROTHESAY DRIVE, GT.CROSBY (to Endbutt Lane)
2387	1934 P	BROWNMOOR LANE (to Northern Road)
2388		THE NORTHERN ROAD
2389		VICARAGE FARM, GREAT CROSBY (portrait)
2390		MARLDON AVENUE, GREAT CROSBY
2392	1934 P	BLUNDELLSANDS STN. (exterior & Serpentine South)
2394	1934 P	WARREN ROAD (from Bridge Road)
2395	1934 P	MERRILOCKS ROAD
2396	*1932*	*CANAL BRIDGE, LITHERLAND (from Church Road)*
		- see illustration opposite.
2399		CHURCH ROAD, LITHERLAND
2401		ST.PHILLIPS AVENUE, LITHERLAND
2402		MOOR LANE, GREAT CROSBY
2403		AMOS AVENUE, LITHERLAND
2404		OXFORD AVENUE, LITHERLAND
2405		HATTON HILL ROAD, LITHERLAND
2406		ALEXANDRA PARK, GREAT CROSBY
2407	*1932*	*COLLEGE ROAD (& 'Corona' cinema) - see illus. opposite.*
2414		LITTLE CROSBY ROAD (north by Mayfair Avenue)
2415	1936 P	RECREATION GROUND, GREAT CROSBY
2416	1936 P	MOORSIDE ROAD (builder's notice - 'new homes £650')
2417	1936 P	THE NORTHERN ROAD
2418	1936 P	LITTLE CROSBY ROAD (to Crosby village)
2419		MERCHANT TAYLORS BOYS SCHOOL, GT.CROSBY
2420		BLUNDELLSANDS SHORE (tents pitched)

Of Cabbages and Kings....

(right) Cushing was no doubt contracted to record this specially built 'Sanitary Car', the unique aspect being the ability to tip and tilt the cover simultaneously without removing same. Devised by Wm. Taylor, wheelwrights, of 13 Little Crosby Road, it became known as 'Taylor's patent'. The handcart version is also shown. (both courtesy of Bob Wright)

(below) Edward, Prince of Wales, visited Crosby on 5th July, 1921 and this is one of at least four cards issued by Stephen Cushing to mark the event. Taken at Islington and Liverpool Road, note the number of ladies in the crowd - then only 27, the future Edward VIII was the most eligible bachelor in the land and still many years from his association with Wallis Simpson and the scandalous abdication which ensued. The un-used condition of this card, tell-tale corner indents and inked cross all confirm that the purchaser noted her presence in the crowd before committing it to an album.

2421	1936 P	BLUNDELLSANDS SHORE (tents pitched)	
2425		HYTHE AVENUE, LITHERLAND	
L 11		CANAL BRIDGE, LITHERLAND (from Church Road)	
L 18		LONGHOUSE FARM	
L 19	1907 P	SEFTON STREET, LITHERLAND	
L 29		BIT OF OLD LITHERLAND	
M 037		ORIEL ROAD, BOOTLE	
M 072		ELM ROAD, SEAFORTH	
M 241	*1910 P*	*KNOWSLEY ROAD, BOOTLE - see illustration page 24.*	
M 301	1909 P	MERTON ROAD, BOOTLE	
M 0117		ALEXANDRA PARK, GREAT CROSBY	
M 0130	1908 P	BLUNDELLSANDS & CROSBY STATION	
M 1106	1908 P	DERBY ROAD, BOOTLE (Bootle Hospital)	
T 12		YORK AVENUE, CROSBY	
T 16		FIVE LAMPS, WATERLOO (& tram)	
T 32	1921 P	ROCKLAND ROAD, WATERLOO	
T 35		CROSBY ROAD NORTH, WATERLOO (& tram)	
T 39	1921 P	SHORE, WATERLOO (& Royal Hotel)	
T 45		POTTER'S BARN	

T 50		CROSBY MILL (close)
T 53		MERRILOCKS ROAD, BLUNDELLSANDS
T 54	*1912 P*	*CORONATION ROAD (shop arcade) - see illus. page 8.*
T 56	1912 P	BRIDGE ROAD, BRIGHTON LE SANDS
T 73	1912 P	COLLEGE ROAD (Carnegie Library)
T 76		CROSBY CONGREGATIONAL CHURCH
T 77		ST. JOHNS ROAD, WATERLOO
T 78	1912 P	WINDMILL, CROSBY (close-up)
T 80		COOKS ROAD, CROSBY (tram terminus)
T 81	1912 P	COOKS ROAD, CROSBY (thatched cottages)
T 82	1922 P	MERRILOCKS ROAD, BLUNDELLSANDS
T 84		CORONATION ROAD, GREAT CROSBY
T 91		BOULDER STONE & ISLINGTON, CROSBY
T 95		(DUPLICATE NUMBER - SEE 1232)
T 98	1912 P	BLUNDELLSANDS HOTEL
T 103		BLUNDELLSANDS ROAD WEST
T 104	1912 P	BLUNDELLSANDS STATION (& electric train)
T 108		GREAT CROSBY COUNCIL SCHOOL
T 112	1912 P	YORK AVENUE
T 113		CHURCH OF ST. PETER & ST. PAUL
T 117		'SOUTHESK' & EROSION, BLUNDELLSANDS
T 118	1912 P	(DUPLICATE NUMBER - SEE 1197)
T 119		(DUPLICATE NUMBER - SEE 1198)
T 120		(DUPLICATE NUMBER - SEE 1200)
T 121		'SOUTHESK', 'BUENA VISTA' & 'NETHERWOOD'
T 134		SEFTON SCHOOLS
T 144	1922 P	SCHOOL LANE, INCE BLUNDELL
T 145		INCE WOODS (1)
T 146		WATER STREET, THORNTON
T 147	1912 P	THORNTON STOCKS

A facsimile Crosby Herald advert from Saturday, 5th January, 1907 and a letterhead from 1924 - it will be noted that neither make reference to picture postcards.

Plus 60 subjects (at the time of writing) taken in other districts including Aintree, Fazakerley, Orrell Park, Walton, Tuebrook, Old Swan Fairfield, Kirkby and Aigburth - see Liverpool North volume for details.

CROSBY ROAD N
WATERLOO

(opposite page) Apart from the area between Dean & Queen Streets, the 1906 map of Waterloo is not too far removed from today's plan. The landscaped gardens which front Marine and Adelaide Terraces were still more than twenty years from construction but the road layout was well and truly established. Detail differences include the footbridge which spanned the railway linking Walmer Road with Hougomont Avenue, the loss of mews properties behind Brunswick Parade and some demolition in Cross Street (behind South Road). The goods & coal yard in Brighton Road has also been consigned to history so too the small precinct of shops which once stood between there and the station. Recent losses have been the English Presbyterian Church and Hall at the junction of Crosby Road South and Great Georges Road together with the nearby Christ Church School (latterly known as Waterloo Grammar School).

(above) This pre-1914 6½" x 4¾" enlargement signed by Cushing on the back, shows the Shelter which once stood by the 'Liver' Hotel. The clarity suggests it was 'contact' printed from a large negative and he is known to have used photographs of this size as calendar subjects. The caption indicates it was also issued as a postcard and note that the positioning of same allowed 5½" x 3½" cards to be produced similarly. This was a common practise and whilst practical for mass production, it denied appreciation of the whole image - a Feilden example is described on page 49.

(right) Having returned from a 100 year exile in the USA, this card shows Cambridge Road, Seaforth around 1905 and the original property that stood between Rawson Road and the one-time junction with Gladstone Road in the distance - the shop on the corner is Roberts' Bros. grocers at No.150 Rawson Road (Cushing No.341).

CAMBRIDGE ROAD
341

WATERLOO

SEAFORTH U.D.

WATERLOO 1906

23

(right) Card No.1943 in the Cushing portfolio shows Seaforth Road from a point just north of the Stella Picture House around 1922. Seaforth Vale North is off to the right with Hicks Road just visible left of the bank. In the distance, the railway station bridge can be seen together with Olswang's tailors and the small parade of shops between there and the gates of the coal & goods yard. These premises have long been demolished and the site is now occupied by a car-park.

SEAFORTH ROAD
SEAFORTH

1943

(left) This Cushing 'M' series card of circa 1910 depicts Knowsley Road, Bootle, between Gray & Dryden Streets. Left to right are Blackledge's bread (112), Clare's fent dealer (110), Rossiter's chandlers (108), Brown's newsagent (106), Roberts' chemist & post-office (104), River Plate Fresh Meat Co. (102), Teire's greengrocers (100) and Slinger's grocers (98). Part of this block suffered in the blitz but the whole site was eventually levelled and redeveloped.

(opposite page) This map of Seaforth in 1906 bears witness to the changes that have taken place particularly in the area south of Church Road and the shore-line.

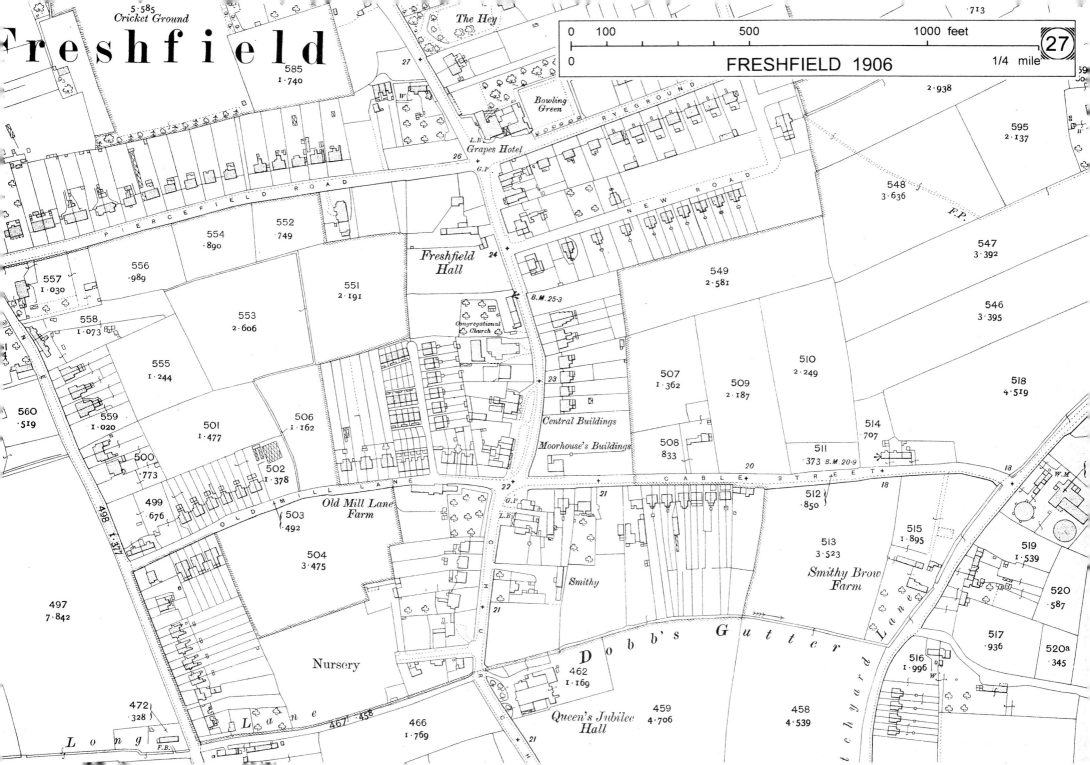

(left) The shops that stood where The Bypass now junctions Liverpool Road are featured here in this Cushing view taken circa 1927. Had this enlargement not come from the family, the absence of any caption would have caused it to go un-noticed. As no postcards have surfaced, I doubt it was ever published - a subject of this kind would have been considered unworthy then. As Borough Photographer, Stephen was most likely instructed to record their existence before demolition - note the presence of workmen and temporary road sign. Langan's Place can be seen by the hanging lamp and the last identities of the shops were (left to right) Sargeant's fish & chips (41), Millet's confectionery (43), Ashton's hairdressers (45) Anwyl's news (47), Ford's drapers (49) and Parsons' chandlers (51). The buildings were swept away soon afterwards but the bypass was not put in until the 1960's.

(right) Recorded as being photographed by Stephen Cushing on 4th May 1912, this postcard of Moor Lane looking towards Liverpool Road shows the full extent of shops present at that time. Apart from the post-office and his own stationery shop far left (Nos. 2 & 4), the only other business premises were on the right and numbered as follows (left to right)

1. Harrington's funerals
3. Wilson's cow-keepers (dairy)
5. Stringfellow's grocery
7. Naylor's upholsterers
9. Eastman's butchers
11. Hurst's chemist
13. Plumer's bakery
15. Wanstall's fruiterers

A Seaforth bound tram can also be seen in the distance having just passed the original 'George Hotel'.

COAST EROSION BLUNDELLSANDS 1878

RIVER ALT HIGHTOWN 1807

CUSHING

Coastal Erosion at Blundellsands. This coastline was the scene of a bitter three-way battle between nature, householders and the council for more than thirty years. The mouth of the River Alt further north has meandered over the years and around 1900 began to spill into the Mersey in a southerly direction. Although the Alt was not suspected to be the cause at the time, the first signs of erosion were noted in 1906. By 1910, it was being taken seriously as 10 yards per annum succumbed to the tides - many houses lay in it's path and worried owners began lobbying the council to build defences. Privately built walls proved useless and by 1927 the sea was threatening homes on Burbo Bank Road North and The Serpentine, which when built in 1888, stood seventy yards from the high water mark. Fearing the remedy was beyond their purse, local officialdom distanced itself and allowed twelve properties to perish before decisive action was taken in 1935. A mile long trolley railway was built from Hall Road West and used to dump tin-slag (from a Bootle smelters) along a 770 yard stretch of the beach. A year later this ten feet rampart was giving cause for celebration and much relief when studies of the Alt's flow showed it to be diverting away from the Blundellsands shore.

In Cushing's card No. 1878 of 1920 (top left) the remains of the most northerly house 'Southesk' are being dismantled by workmen rather than allow it to become a total loss. In No. 2022 of 1923 (top middle) 'Holmside' teeters dangerously on the brink but the presence of washing on the line suggests the owners were hopeful of a last minute reprieve. (Top right) The alleged culprit, the River Alt at Hightown as depicted in Cushing's No. 1807 view - Formby Lighthouse is also just visible on the horizon.

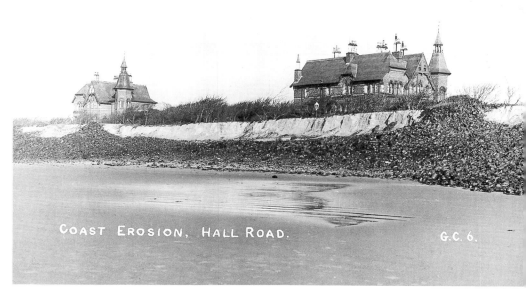

COAST EROSION, HALL ROAD. G.C. 6.

 Feilden's GC 6 card of 1935 (above) portrays the action taken by the council with spills of tin-slag. The chapter on this photographer's work begins overleaf.

B & A FEILDEN

Brothers Basil and Alan Feilden were self-taught photographers who operated from the family home of 12 Harlech Road, Blundellsands. Born in 1908 and 1912 respectively, they were natives of the Bradford area and moved with their parents to 2 Coronation Road, Crosby, some time around 1914. Their father, Herbert, was a manufacturer's agent for the Sheffield firm of Pickering's who made polish.

They were resident at Harlech Road by 1918 and Basil took an immediate interest in matters maritime which was no doubt helped by father taking him to the Crosby shore to witness the first Mersey sailing of the liner 'Aquitania' on 30th May 1914 - in later life he could still recall the smell of it's smoke and noise of the siren.

As the brothers grew older they shared a love of photography and by 1929 Basil combined his two interests by taking pictures of ships - a diary for that year notes that he took 78 photographs of various vessels. The next two years detail 126 & 232 exposures respectively and these figures plus the snowball of demand most likely steered him towards professional status.

With regard to other views, apart from random exposures in 1929 and seven shots taken at the Liverpool & Manchester Railway Centenary celebrations at Wavertree Playground in 1930, their inland coverage only began in earnest following opening day pictures of the Mersey road tunnel in 1934. Cards of their early efforts may never have circulated as none have been traced and the earliest known post-mark for an inland issue corresponds with the opening of the tunnel. Their 'LV' (Liverpool) series was soon followed by a host of others - GC for the Crosby area, W for Waterloo, LS for Litherland &

Seaforth, B for Bootle, BH for Birkenhead, WS for Wallasey & Seacombe and SP for Southport. No street scenes were taken beyond 1939 as far as can be determined.

 Basil Feilden pictured in his RAF days. (photo courtesy of Christine Hamer)

Thankfully, the mainland portfolio also received numbers, a practise that was not generally applied to their shipping subjects even though four-page brochures were issued for same.

Basil usually travelled on foot and by bus but in 1937 he purchased a motorcycle to get about on - a New Imperial 350cc to which he strapped his Ensign de luxe reflex camera. In order to gain access to subjects on the river, he possessed a tug pass and would often endure poor weather to capture his prey - no mean feat on a rolling and slippery deck. Their maritime list will appear

in a future volume as will views from other areas.

Being the consummate professional that he was, Basil recorded each exposure in his diaries (two pages of one being reproduced opposite). Whilst these proved useful in dating many subjects, he took so many variations at different periods it has not been possible to match them all - the diary negative numbers bearing no relation to those applied to the post-cards. Frustrating though this was, it was more than compensated for by the discovery of 90% of the Feilden negatives, the majority being in excellent condition.

This treasure trove filled many gaps in the list and unearthed an entire hitherto unknown series - the 'SP' subjects. At the time of writing no Feilden issues of Southport have surfaced and it must be assumed that these cards were never marketed. With no mention of them in Basil's diaries (1929-1938), they were most likely taken in the summer of 1939 and the intervention of the second world war probably explains why they never appeared. Although the town is outside the intended area of this volume, the circumstances surrounding these 'cards that never were' dictate their inclusion, if only for posterity - see illustration on rear cover.

The discovery of the 6½" x 4¾" negatives also revealed that the cards were 'contact' printed as opposed to being enlarged from smaller format celluloid. As a result, up to half an inch of subject matter per side is absent on the post-cards.

Thanks to surviving records, it was relatively easy to determine the size of the brothers' portfolio by 1939 - including ships, it was approximately 1600. Both men made life-time careers of photography - Alan, who usually took a back-seat in the postcard venture, was a RAF photographer in India during the war and later worked for the renowned commercial photographers, Stewart Bale Ltd. Basil's war service was also spent in the RAF but as an air frame fitter which suited his other skills - metalworking and engineering. He resumed photography in 1950 and advertised his wares in *'Sea Breezes'* and other journals but finally gave up a decade later. He moved to Southport in the early fifties and died there in 1995 - brother Alan surviving him by a year.

Cards can be bordered or borderless but all are regular black and white issues. Most are stamped 'Copyright B. & A. Feilden, Blundellsands, Liverpool 23' on the reverse but those that escaped this process are usually identifiable on the obverse by virtue of their distinctive captions and superb quality. Note that the Feildens' Liverpool (LV), Birkenhead (BH), Wallasey & Seacombe (WS) & Shipping (S) (SV) series will feature in later volumes. (Biography courtesy of John Clarkson)

(above) Taken from a 1954 edition of 'Sea Breezes', this Feilden advert shows that Basil's portfolio of shipping titles increased year on year - the 1200 advertised in 1939 had doubled fifteen years later (courtesy of 'Sea Breezes').

(right upper) Facing pages of Basil Feilden's 1936 diary for the 10th June with times and details of each subject. Sadly, these jottings were never cross-referenced with the actual card numbers and as he visited many sites more than once, it is impossible to marry-up the majority. However, some exposures were unique and these allow the inclusion of such reference numbers - seven being shown here to the right of the relevant entries. (courtesy of John Clarkson)

(right lower) A Feilden Brothers letter-head from the 1930's clearly indicating that maritime work was the mainstay of their business.

| Date | No. of Slide | Plate or Film | EXPOSURE RECORDS | | | OR MEMORANDA | No. of Negative | |
			Time of Day	Light	Stop	Exposure	Subject, notes on lighting, etc.	
10/6/36	N°.4	SS Pan	11.35 AM		f.16	1/5 sec	Pleasure Float 37 min fo	✓	
"	N°.5	"	11.45 AM	"	f.22	1/5	Dowhills Road Pleasure Flate	✓	
"	N°.6	"	11.50 AM	"	f.11	25 sec	Dowhills Road	"	✓ GC 40
"	M°.7	"	12 Noon	"	f.11	25 sec	Dowhills + St Anthony's Road	"	✓ GC 42
"	N°.8	"	12.25 PM	"	f.11,16	25 sec	Estra Road North	"	✓ GC 38
"	N°.9	"	12.35 PM	"	f.11	25 sec	St Michaels	"	✓ GC 45
"	N°.10	"	12.50 PM	"	f.11	25 sec	College Road North	"	✓ GC 44
"	N°.11	"	1.20 PM	"	f.11	25 sec	Grey's Hotel	"	✓
"	N°.12	"	1.20 PM	"	f.11	25 sec	Crown Buildings	"	✓ GC 37
"	N°.13	"	3.12 PM	"	f.16	25 sec	Marine Gardens 32 min: Tank Reflect	✓	
"	N°.11	"	3.20 PM	"	f.11,16	25 sec	" " 32 " "	✓	
"	N°.10	"	3.28 PM	"	f.11,16	25 sec	" " (Pond) " "	✓ W 38	
"	N°.9	"	3.30 PM	"	f.11,16	25 sec	" " " "	✓	

PHOTOGRAPHS SUPPLIED TO:—
SHIPPING COMPANIES
SHIPBUILDERS,
MANUFACTURERS,
PUBLISHERS,
STATIONERY TRADE,
COLLECTORS. Etc.

B. & A. FEILDEN,
12, HARLECH ROAD,
Blundellsands, LIVERPOOL, 23.
MARINE AND COMMERCIAL PHOTOGRAPHY

REFERENCES

YOURS   OURS

BRIDGE ROAD, LITHERLAND. L.S.I.

(below) Stanley Road, Bootle (B4) was taken on the same day as the accompanying view - 20th March 1935. Part of North Recreation Ground can be seen left whilst the right foreground is occupied by St. Matthews church - still a place of worship today. The nearby junctions are Hornby Road which once formed a crossroads here and skirted two perimeters of the park - see map on Page 57.

(above) Bridge Road, Litherland, with it's recently built lift-bridge was Feilden's choice for card No.1 in the Litherland and Seaforth series. Taken on 20th March 1935, compare this to the view taken thirty one years earlier on Page 72. The shop at the corner of Jubilee Road, is Arnold's confectioners (No.117) and amongst the placards there are publicity bills for the 'Coliseum' picture house which stood on Linacre Road, a few hundred yards away. On the extreme right, Hardman & Co., motor engineers, of No.3 Linacre Road can be seen together with two petrol pumps, one of which bears a 'National Benzole' globe - a popular brand that remained so for another thirty years or more. To the left of the garage is Armstrong's Removals at No.1 Linacre Road.

STANLEY ROAD, BOOTLE. B.4.

FEILDEN B & A

No.	Date	Location or Subject

(D) Denotes a Diary entry only with no known surviving negative or postcard to indicate a series number - see biography.

No.	Date	Location or Subject
(D)	20-3-35	CHRIST CHURCH, BOOTLE
B 1	20-3-35	STANLEY ROAD, BOOTLE (near Merton Road)
B 2	20-3-35	STANLEY ROAD, BOOTLE (near Balliol Road) - see illustration Page 42
B 3	20-3-35	KING'S GARDENS, STANLEY ROAD, BOOTLE
B 4	20-3-35	STANLEY ROAD, BOOTLE (near Hornby Road) - see illustration opposite
B 5	20-3-35	KNOWSLEY RD, BOO. (Gainsborough Cinema) - see illustration Page 49
B 6	20-3-35	MERTON ROAD, BOOTLE (near Stanley Road)
B 7	20-3-35	WAR MEMORIAL, BOOTLE
B 8	20-3-35	BALLIOL ROAD, BOOTLE (near Public Baths)
B 9	20-3-35	MUNICIPAL BLDGS, ORIEL ROAD - see illus. Page 42
~		THE SHORE, CROSBY (Mariners Road - no caption / No.)
~		THE SHORE,.CROSBY (bathers - no caption or No.)
(D)	24-8-29	LANDMARK, BLUNDELLSANDS SHORE
(D)	1930 C	SEFTON CHURCH (4 Negs between 2-1930 & 5-1931)
(D)	5-1930	SERPENTINE, B/SANDS (depositing clinker)
(D)	5-1930	SERPENTINE, BLUNDELLSANDS (road & erosion)
(D)	12-1930	INCE BLUNDELL PARK
(D)	3-1935	ST.HELENS CHURCH, GREAT CROSBY
(D)	10-6-36	GEORGE HOTEL, CROSBY
GC 1	1-1935	TOWN HALL, GT CROSBY
GC 2	1-1935	CARNEGIE LIBRARY, GT CROSBY
GC 3		WAR MEMORIAL, GT CROSBY
GC 4	3-1935	CONGREGATIONAL CHURCH, CROSBY (Mersey Road)
GC 5	3-1935	ST.LUKE'S CHURCH, GT CROSBY
GC 6		COAST EROSION, HALL ROAD - see illustration Page 29
GC 7		COAST EROSION, HALL ROAD (from road)
GC 8	3-1935	THE MILL, GT CROSBY (Moor Lane)
GC 9	3-1935	MERCHANT TAYLORS SCHOOL
GC 11	3-1935	ST MICHAEL'S WELL, GT CROSBY - see illus. Page 34
GC 12	1939 P	ALEXANDRA HALL, GT CROSBY - see illus. Page 46
GC 14	12-6-35	CROSBY COUNCIL SCHOOL (Coronation Road)
GC 15	12-6-35	COLLEGE ROAD, GT CROSBY (near Warwick Avenue) - see illustration Page 36
GC 16	12-6-35	LIVERPOOL ROAD, GT. CROSBY (near Endbutt Lane)
GC 17		THE VILLAGE, GT CROSBY (Moor Lane to Cooks Road) - see illustration Page 44
GC 19	12-6-35	ALEXANDRA PARK, GT CROSBY
GC 21		THE SHORE, CROSBY (tents pitched)
GC 23	12-6-35	RECREATION GROUND, GT CROSBY (bowlers)
GC 24		CROWN BUILDINGS, GREAT CROSBY
GC 28		THE SHORE, CROSBY (Mariners Road)
GC 29	1935 P	THE SHORE, CROSBY - see illustration Page 45
GC 30	4-9-35	MODEL YACHT POND, GT. CROSBY
GC 31	12-6-35	RECREATION GROUND, GT. CROSBY
GC 32	4-9-35	ENDBUTT LANE CORNER, GT. CROSBY (Liverpool Rd.) - see illustration Page 46
GC 33	4-9-35	CORONATION ROAD, GT. CROSBY (from Carnegie Ave.) - see illustration Page 36
GC 34	12-6-35	ALEXANDRA PARK, GT. CROSBY
GC 35	12-6-35	ALEXANDRA PARK, GT. CROSBY (path & lady)
GC 36	12-6-35	ALEXANDRA PARK, GT. CROSBY (family seated)
GC 37	10-6-36	CROWN BUILDINGS, GT. CROSBY (from Liverpool Road)
GC 38	10-6-36	ESHE ROAD NORTH, BLUNDELLSANDS
GC 39	1937 P	THE VILLAGE, GT. CROSBY (from Islington)
GC 40	10-6-36	DOWHILLS ROAD, BLUNDELLSANDS
GC 41	9-6-36	WARREN ROAD, BLUNDELLSANDS
GC 42	10-6-36	DOWHILLS & ST. ANTHONYS RD, BLUNDELLSANDS
GC 43	9-6-36	BRIDGE ROAD, BLUNDELLSANDS - see illus. Page 45
GC 44	10-6-36	COLLEGE ROAD NORTH, BLUNDELLSANDS
GC 45	10-6-36	ST. MICHAEL'S CHURCH, BLUNDELLSANDS
GC 46	10-6-36	BLUNDELLSANDS HOTEL (portrait format)
GC 47	10-6-36	BLUNDELLSANDS HOTEL (landscape format)
(G)C 48		CROSBY SHORE (paddlers) - Numbered C 48 only.
(G)C 49		CROSBY SHORE (crowd posing)
(G)C 49		RECREATION GROUND, GT CROSBY (swing-park)
(G)C 50		RECREATION GROUND, GT CROSBY (swing-park)
(G)C 50		CROSBY SHORE (crowd paddling)
(G)C 51		MODEL YACHT POND, CROSBY
(G)C 52	4-9-35	ALEXANDRA PARK, CROSBY (boy on path)
(G)C 53	4-9-35	RECREATION GROUND, CROSBY (boulder stone)
(G)C 54	4-9-35	ALEXANDRA PARK, CROSBY
(G)C 56	4-9-35	ALEXANDRA PARK, CROSBY
(G)C 57	4-9-35	RECREATION GROUND, CROSBY
(G)C 58		ALEXANDRA PARK, CROSBY (man seated)
LS 1	20-3-35	BRIDGE ROAD, LITHERLAND - see illustration opposite
LS 2	3-1935	SEAFORTH ROAD, SEAFORTH (& 'Palladium' cinema) - see illustration Page 40
LS 3	3-1935	ST THOMAS'S CHURCH, SEAFORTH
LS 4	9-4-35	BRIDGE ROAD, LITHERLAND (Eaton Ave. to Linacre Rd.) - see illustration Page 40
LS 5	9-4-35	LITHERLAND PARK, LITHERLAND
LS 6	9-4-35	COUNCIL OFFICES, LITHERLAND
LS 7	9-4-35	ROCK GARDEN, LITHERLAND PARK, LITHERLAND
LS 8	9-4-35	ST PHILIP'S CHURCH, LITHERLAND
LS 9	9-4-35	WAR MEMORIAL, LITHERLAND
LS 10	9-4-35	ROCK GDN, L/LAND PK, LITHERLAND (& tennis courts)
LS 11	9-4-35	CHURCH OF THE ENGLISH MARTYRS, LITHERLAND
LS 12	3-1935	LINACRE RD, LITHERLAND (Stanley & Knowsley Roads) - see illustration Page 48
LS 13	3-1935	LINACRE ROAD, LITHERLAND (from Croxteth Road)

ST MICHAEL'S WELL, GT CROSBY.   G.C.11.

(left) This cross sited in The Green, Crosby Village, marked the position of St. Michael's Well which was once used as a font by a nearby church of that name - Crosby's first place of worship (demolished 1864). The Festival of the Cross was held every St.Michael's day on 29th September when it was festooned with flowers - games were also played on the village green (a triangle of land that became the police station but is now part of Sainsbury's supermarket). This March 1935 view shows the Moor Place opening with Brenning's pawnbrokers and Myerscough's butchers either side of same - although this alley still exists, it once led to a terrace of twelve cottages (see map on Page 9). Note also that the old 'Crosby Vaults' building, left of the railings, had been converted to shops by then.

(right) If other 1930's Feilden views are anything to go by, this has to be considered rush-hour on Crosby Road, Waterloo - the position of the long shadows also indicate it was taken one evening and most likely in 1936. Note that the five lamps monument was a true traffic island then with northbound vehicles from Great Georges Road able to pass it on the left hand side. The approaching bus is a Ribble 'L1' Crosby service from Liverpool - the route being Stanley Road, Linacre Road, Seaforth Road, Church Road, Crosby Road, College Road and Victoria Road.

FIVE LAMPS, WATERLOO.   W.45.

SP 1*	1939 C	MARINE LAKE & PIER, SOUTHPORT
SP 2*	1939 C	SHORE & MARINE LAKE, SOUTHPORT
SP 3*	1939 C	KING'S GARDENS, SOUTHPORT
SP 4*	1939 C	KING'S GARDENS, SOUTHPORT (bowlers)
SP 5*	1939 C	MODEL YACHT POND, SOUTHPORT
SP 6*	1939 C	KING'S GARDENS, SOUTHPORT (to promenade)
*SP 7**	*1939 C*	*THE WATER CHUTE, PLEASURELAND, SOUTHPORT*
		- see illustration rear cover.
SP 8*	1939 C	SEA BATHING LAKE, SOUTHPORT
SP 9*	1939 C	MARINE LAKE, SOUTHPORT (north to pier)
SP 10*	1939 C	SEA BATHING LAKE, SOUTHPORT
SP 11*	1939 C	BOATING & PADDLING POOLS, MARINE LAKE, S/PORT
SP 12*	1939 C	SHORE & MARINE LAKE, SOUTHPORT
SP 13*	1939 C	BOATING & PADDLING POOLS, MARINE LAKE, S/PORT
SP 14*	1939 C	SEA BATHING LAKE, SOUTHPORT
SP 15*	1939 C	SEA BATHING LAKE, SOUTHPORT (& divers)
SP 16*	1939 C	MARINE LAKE, SOUTHPORT (& bridge)
SP 17*	1939 C	MARINE LAKE, SOUTHPORT (bridge close-up)
SP 18*	1939 C	LAKE, HESKETH PARK, SOUTHPORT (& swans)
SP 19*	1939 C	LAKE, HESKETH PARK, SOUTHPORT
SP 20*	1939 C	LAKE, HESKETH PARK, SOUTHPORT
SP 21*	1939 C	HESKETH PARK, SOUTHPORT (children & pram)
SP 22*	1939 C	HESKETH PARK, SOUTHPORT (lake & swan)
SP 23*	1939 C	PROMENADE, SOUTHPORT (looking north)
SP 24*	1939 C	SEA BATHING LAKE, SOUTHPORT
SP 25*	1939 C	SPEEDBOATS, PLEASURELAND, SOUTHPORT
SP 26*	1939 C	SEA BATHING LAKE, SOUTHPORT (& onlookers)
SP 27*	1939 C	SEA BATHING LAKE, SOUTHPORT (3 feet end)
SP 28*	1939 C	MARINE LAKE, SOUTHPORT (& two bridges)

* SP series believed never issued due to outbreak of Second World War.

~	5-1930	R100 AIRSHIP OVER WATERLOO (No number or caption)
W 1		MARINE GARDENS, WATERLOO (& Royal Hotel)
W 2		MARINE GARDENS, WATERLOO (to Marine Terrace)
W 3	3-1935	CROSBY ROAD SOUTH, WATERLOO (north fr. 5 Lamps)
W 4	3-1935	SOUTH ROAD, WATERLOO (east from Lorne Road)
W 5	*3-1935*	*SOUTH ROAD, WATERLOO (& 'Queens' cinema)*
		- see illustration Page 47
W 6	3-1935	FIVE LAMPS, WATERLOO (portrait format)
W 7		*ST JOHNS ROAD, WATERLOO (east from Ferndale Road)*
		- see illustration Page 38
W 8		MARINE GARDENS, WATERLOO
W 9		ADELAIDE GARDENS, WATERLOO (to river)
W 10	18-3-35	MERSEY VIEW, WATERLOO (from Oxford Road)
W 11	*18-3-35*	*OXFORD RD, W/LOO (from Manley Rd.) - see ill. Page 48*
W 12		ADELAIDE GARDENS, WATERLOO (north & terrace)
W 13		ADELAIDE GARDENS, WATERLOO (north & terrace)
W 14		ADELAIDE GARDENS, WATERLOO (to Beach Lawn)
W 15		ADELAIDE GARDENS, WATERLOO (steps & terrace)
W 16		ADELAIDE GARDENS, WATERLOO (steps & river)
W 17		ADELAIDE GARDENS, WATERLOO (north & river)

W 18		MARINE GARDENS, WATERLOO (to Royal Hotel)
W 19		ADELAIDE TERRACE, WATERLOO
W 20	23-4-35	LEOPOLD ROAD, WATERLOO (from river)
W 21	23-4-35	HEATHFIELD ROAD, WATERLOO (from river)
W 22	12-4-35	ST FAITH'S CHURCH, WATERLOO (Milton Road side)
W 23		THE SHORE, WATERLOO (south with crowd posing)
W 24		THE SHORE, WATERLOO (west with crowd posing)
W 25	*26-7-35*	*VICTORIA PK, W/LOO (from footbridge) - see ill. Page 38*
W 26	26-7-35	VICTORIA PARK, WATERLOO (to Lawton Road)
W 27	26-7-35	VICTORIA PARK, WATERLOO
W 28	26-7-35	VICTORIA PARK, WATERLOO (& pavilion)
W 29		WATERLOO & SEAFORTH GRAMMAR SCHOOL, W/LOO
W 30	29-3-35	BROOKE ROAD WEST, WATERLOO (from river)
W 31		ADELAIDE GARDENS, WATERLOO (south & steps)
W 32		ADELAIDE GARDENS, WATERLOO (to Beach Lawn)
W 33		ADELAIDE GARDENS, WATERLOO (north & river)
W 34		ADELAIDE GARDENS, WATERLOO (to terrace)
W 35		ADELAIDE GARDENS, WATERLOO (north & terrace)
W 36		ADELAIDE GARDENS, WATERLOO (south & river)
W 37		MARINE GARDENS, WATERLOO (to Royal Hotel)
W 38	10-6-36	MARINE GARDENS, WATERLOO (pond)
W 39		MARINE GARDENS, WATERLOO (north & river)
W 40		MARINE GARDENS, WATERLOO (south & Royal Hotel)
W 41		MARINE GARDENS, WATERLOO (north & terrace)
W 42	10-6-36	ROYAL HOTEL, WATERLOO (from Marine Gardens)
W 43		CRESCENT GARDEN, WATERLOO (south & river)
W 44		CRESCENT GARDEN, WATERLOO (north & fountain)
W 45		*FIVE LAMPS, WATERLOO (south to Crosby Road South)*
		- see illustration opposite
W 46		CRESCENT GARDEN, WATERLOO (north & river)
W 47		CRESCENT GARDEN, WATERLOO (to river)
W 48		CRESCENT GARDEN, WATERLOO (to river)
W 49		CRESCENT GARDEN, WATERLOO (& Marine Crescent)
W 50		CRESCENT GARDEN, WATERLOO (to Marine Crescent)
W 51		CRESCENT GARDEN, WATERLOO (& steps)
W 52		CRESCENT GARDEN, WATERLOO (north & Marine Cres)
W 53		CRESCENT GARDEN, WATERLOO (& fountain)
W 53		WATERLOO SHORE (river & paddlers)
W 54		WATERLOO SHORE (river & paddlers)
W 54		CRESCENT GARDEN, WATERLOO (south overall)
W 55		CRESCENT GARDEN, WATERLOO (south to river)
W 56		CRESCENT GARDEN, WATERLOO (south)
W 57		BEACH LAWN GARDENS, WATERLOO (footbridge)
W 58		BEACH LAWN GARDENS, WATERLOO (south & river)
W 59		BEACH LAWN GARDENS, WATERLOO (rockery)
W 60		BEACH LAWN GARDENS, WATERLOO (to Beach Lawn)
W 61		BEACH LAWN GARDENS, WATERLOO (to river)
W 62		BEACH LAWN GARDENS, WATERLOO (shelter)
W 63		VICTORIA PARK, WATERLOO (& bowlers)
W 64		VICTORIA PARK, WATERLOO

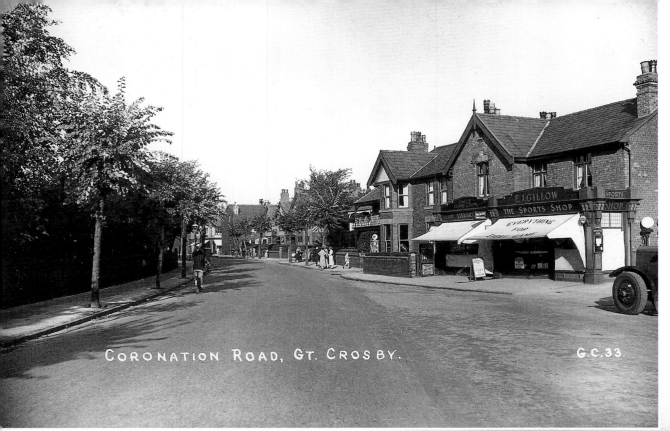

CORONATION ROAD, GT. CROSBY.

G.C.33.

(left)   G.C. 33 in the Great Crosby series recorded something that was close to Basil Feilden's heart - No.2 Coronation Road, which was the family's first home following their move from Bradford. Seen here as Gillow's sports shop on 4th Sept. 1935, the premises were clearly converted for business use some time prior to this. The College Motor Co. is off camera to the right but the neighbouring shop is Corke's confectioners at No.2a or 'Uncle Tom's Cabin' as can be seen. Beyond that is Shaw's at No.4, a coal and haulage firm with their own petrol pump.

(opposite page)   The College Road area was slowly losing it's open spaces by 1925 as this map of the period records - note the allotments on Sunnyside Road, Shrewsbury Avenue under construction and some of the proposed road names and junctions on the development south of Coronation Drive.

(right)   Taken on 12th June 1935, G.C.15 pictures the College Road shops opposite Marine's football ground. Right to left are.....

128	Oliver Pritchard	pork butcher
130	Albert B Shaw	butcher
132	Ellen Corke	stationer
134	Ellen Lawrence	baby linen
136	William H Shaw	hairdresser
	Warwick Avenue	
138	Scott & Sons	bakers
140	Henry Roman	boots & shoes
142	Alice M Mason	confectioner
144	James S Sawyer	ironmonger

Note also the gent sporting a straw boater outside Corke's and the wooden hoardings fronting the football ground covered in advertising bills.

COLLEGE ROAD, GT CROSBY.

G.C.15

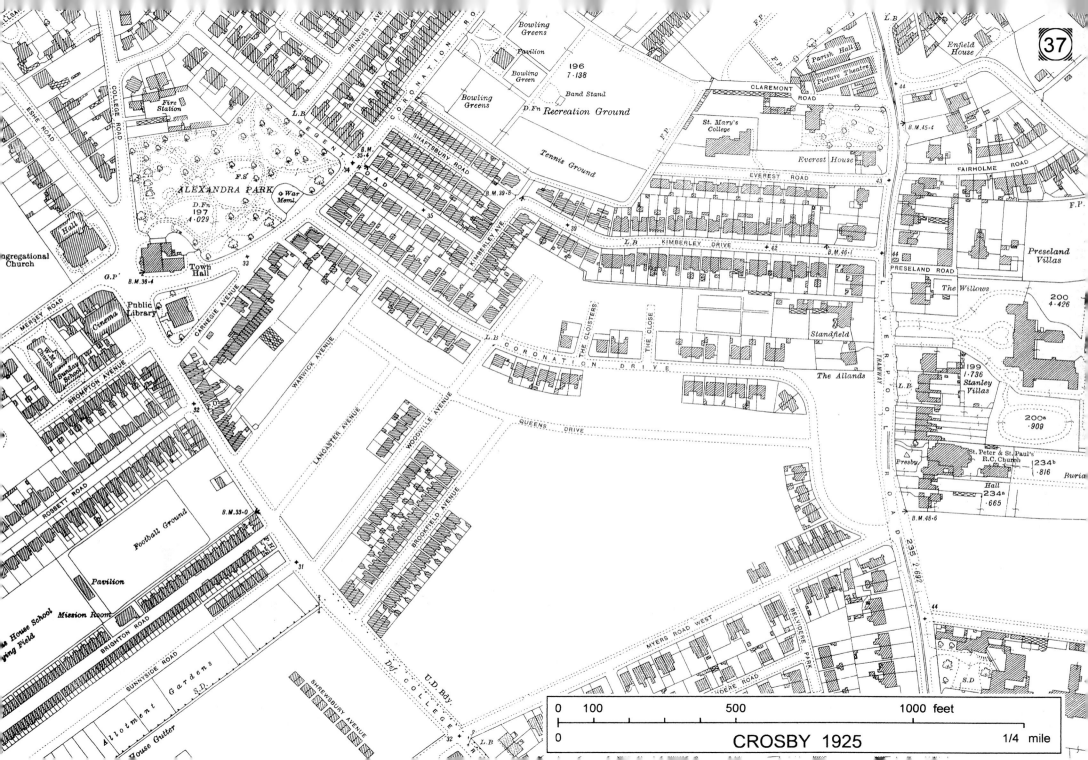

CROSBY 1925

0 100 500 1000 feet

0 1/4 mile

(opposite page)   This 1925 map of the Waterloo St.Johns Road area appears to be no different to today's but close inspection reveals a number of changes. Gone are most of the terraced properties in 'Little Scandinavia' namely Denmark, Sweden & Norway Streets; the railway goods yard in Brighton Road and many of the fine merchant's houses in the vicinity of the present day library. Note also that the way from Somerville Road to Somerville Grove was by footpath and the connection to Manley Road and it's allotments by means of a track-level 'occupation crossing' as they were then known - the footbridge and Somerville Road extension being built some time prior to 1935 (see below).

ST JOHNS ROAD, WATERLOO.   W.7.

VICTORIA PARK, WATERLOO.   W.25.

(above)   Taken from it's junction with Ferndale Road, this view of St. John's Road looks to Crosby Road North. Always having been in the shadow of South Road commercially, this road has long offered a more sedate form of shopping with it's many grocers, butchers and hairdressers. As regards the date, the lack of tree foliage suggests this is another of Feilden's March 1935 exposures.

(left)   With more than a third of his portfolio covering parks and gardens, they were either an obsession of Feilden's or very popular with buyers of postcards - whilst pleasing to the eye, they offer little in historical terms when compared to street scenes. Although far more manicured than it appears today, this July 1935 view of Victoria Park taken from the railway footbridge shows the recently built link road between Somerville Grove and Somerville Road - see the map opposite for the footpath layout which existed prior to this.

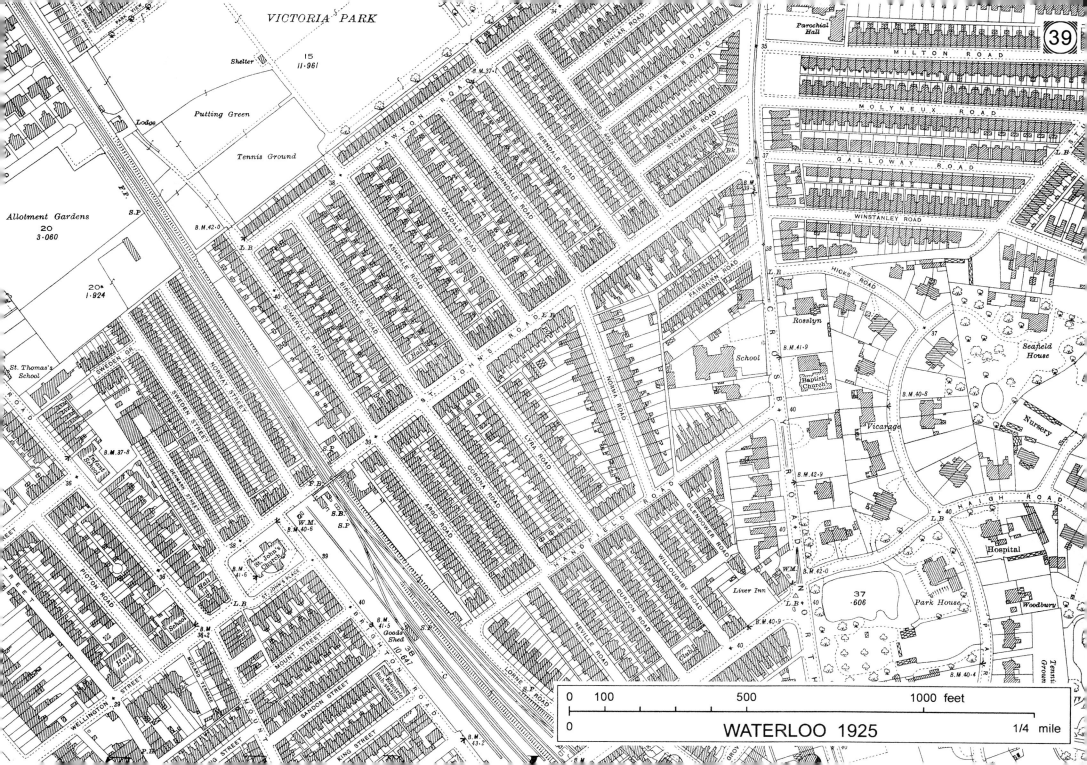

WATERLOO 1925

(right) A view of Bridge Road, Litherland taken from the corner of Hawthorne Grove looking towards the canal bridge. Clearly numbered L.S.4, it was taken on 9th April 1935 as were most of Feilden's Litherland & Seaforth series. Although the area has changed significantly through a combination of world war two bombing and redevelopment, the block on the right between Eaton and Penrhyn Avenues still exists and marks the boundary where the present day shops end and a large traffic island begins. The 1935 directory records that the businesses on that arcade then were (right to left) O'Conner's greengrocers (50), Griffins Cash Chemist (52), Hirschman's drapery (54), British & Argentine Meat Co.Ltd (56), Hammond's confectioners (58), Lawson's bakery (60), Keating's confectioners (62) and Irwin's grocers (64).

BRIDGE ROAD, LITHERLAND.   L.S.4.

SEAFORTH ROAD, SEAFORTH.   L.S.2.

(left) Seaforth Road in March 1935 showing the Palladium cinema - the film 'Stamboul Quest' (1934) was playing that day, a world war one weepie starring Myrna Loy and George Brent. Opening relatively early in 1913, this 905 seater closed it's doors to a declining number of picture-goers in 1959 but still survives as a warehouse. On the left is Bowersdale Park with the area's other cinema, the 'Stella', just visible beyond the trees. Although not opening until 1920, this larger building closed a year before it's competitor and was demolished in 1964 to make way for a shopping precinct of the same name.

(opposite page) This map of Seaforth in 1925 shows the layout of streets before the Princess Way dual carriageway dissected the area and claimed a large number of properties in the process.

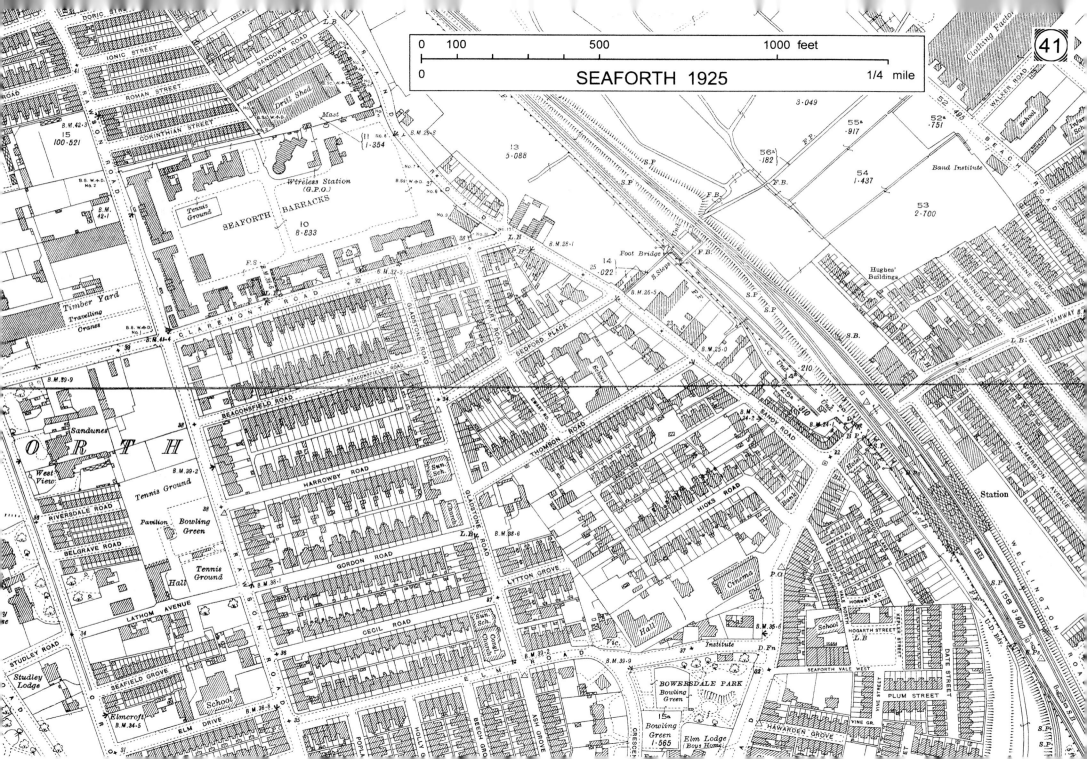

SEAFORTH 1925

41

0 100 500 1000 feet

0 1/4 mile

STANLEY ROAD, BOOTLE.

B.2.

(left) Stanley Road, Bootle on 20th March 1935 with a No.23 Seaforth tram approaching Balliol Road traffic lights - right is the Emmanuel Congregational church which survived the blitz but was demolished in 1965 following a fire.

(opposite page) Whilst the infrastructure of roads has changed little since this 1925 survey of Bootle's Millers Bridge area was drawn, the blitz and socio-economic factors are largely responsible for the numerous detail differences since then. Apart from obvious gaps amongst the dockside warehouses and the skeletal remains of the rail network, the most significant absentees today are the rows of terraced houses off Derby Road and many of the canalside factories which employed their residents - a walk along the towpath of this section then would have revealed a boatbuilder's wharf, a sackworks, a borax refinery and many other manufacturers together with 'teamowners' yards (the term given to horse drawn haulage operators).

(right) Bootle's Municipal Buildings and main post office on 20th March 1935 from Balliol Road. On the left, we can see a glimpse of the area's long forgotten secondary railway station, 'Bootle Balliol Road' - the nameboard is partly visible as is the booking hall beyond. Dwarfed by the larger Oriel Road station, it was on the Alexandra Dock branch and connected the area with the Walton, Tuebrook and Edge Hill districts. Although selling it's last passenger ticket in May 1948, the line is still in use as a link to the Seaforth Container Base.

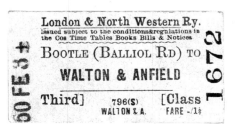

London & North Western Ry.
Issued subject to the conditions&regulations in the Cos Time Tables Books Bills & Notices

BOOTLE (BALLIOL RD) TO

WALTON & ANFIELD

Third]   796(S)   [Class
            WALTON & A.   FARE -/1½

00 FE 3   1672

MUNICIPAL BUILDINGS, ORIEL ROAD, BOOTLE.

B.9.

BOOTLE 1925

THE VILLAGE, GT CROSBY.

Although the exact exposure date of this view is not recorded conclusively, it was probably taken in 1935 like most of the Crosby portfolio. On the right is the 'George Hotel' which was rebuilt six years earlier and undoubtedly to the annoyance of Blackledge's - the taller structure masking most of their gable advertisement. The left hand gable of Davies butchers at No.22 Liverpool Road betrays where the 'Ship Hotel' (No.24) once adjoined - the crude pointing to all except the top portion shows that the front of the property was demolished (circa 1923) and the remainder re-constructed on a building line set further back. The pub was one of two bearing that name in Crosby - the other was at No.17 Warrenhouse Road which pulled it's last pint around 1925.

(left) With the family home no more than a hundred yards away in Harlech Road, Feilden did not travel far to take this view of Bridge Road, Blundellsands, on 9th June 1936. This scene is relatively unchanged except for different street furniture and the addition of a pedestrian crossing further on. As will be seen on most of these views, there was virtually no need for crossings in the thirties. Motor vehicles were relatively scarce and there was far more chance of being struck by a bicycle - despite the few people at large, there are ten bikes to be seen here. The bus near Mariners Road is the old 'L3' operated by Ribble Motor Services which plied between Liverpool and Crosby via Stanley Road, Linacre Road, Sandy Road, Crosby Road, South Road, Oxford Road & Coronation Road.

(right) G.C.29 in the Crosby series shows the beach near Mariners Road and how popular such a venue once was. Notice the dress code - there were no T-shirts or jeans then and the youngsters usually wore open-necked shirts with short trousers. Not so their seniors - they steadfastly refused this attire and turned up in ties, hats and coats together with a case full of sandwiches and the obligatory 'Thermos'. Some would go for a ritual paddle in the river with trousers rolled to the knee but this and showing their braces was as cosmopolitan as most dared to be. The mockery ends here, however - they had a cheap day out, clean beaches, no traffic jams or ghetto blasters, deck-chair hire and patrolling ice-cream vendors. Note the number of tents - they were usually pitched for one of three reasons....Changing into and out of one's 'cozzi'; Shielding the primus stove from the wind; Advanced courtship.

ALEXANDRA HALL, GT CROSBY. G.C.12.

(left) Alexandra Hall was Great Crosby's Town Hall and a feature of College Road for many years until demolition at the beginning of 2004. Many period drama scenes were filmed here in the latter part of the twentieth century owing to the survival of the original police courts within the building. Note the fine lamp with it's 'AA' direction and distance indicators - Blundellsands ¼, Southport 14, Waterloo 1 and Liverpool 6. This view, taken in 1935, has been reproduced from a postcard because of damage to the negative. Telephone kiosks were becoming common to our streets by this year and the type depicted here were painted white (to the left of the Hall).

(right) The art-deco features of this newly completed block at Liverpool Road and Endbutt Lane no doubt persuaded Feilden to include it in their portfolio and so he did on 4th September 1935. Built by local entrepreneur and builder Alexander W. Glenn, his promotional board can be seen on the extreme right - *'shops for sale or freehold'*. Left to right the new traders were Winstanley & Lambert, electrical supplies; Meldon's butchers; Booth's wines; Scott's bakery; Moore's confectioners & newsagent; O'Connor's chemist and Fred's, child's outfitters. The block remains relatively unchanged with all units bar one retaining their fashionable upper storey windows. The similarly designed 'Glenn Buildings' on Moor Lane were also erected by the same builder and he based his offices there - it was also the venue for the local Conservative club and remains so today.

ENDBUTT LANE CORNER, GT. CROSBY. G.C.32.

SOUTH ROAD, WATERLOO.

W.5.

Taken in March 1935, 'W5' of Feildens' Waterloo series looks east along South Road and affords a wonderful view of the 'Queens Picture House' (1913 - 1959). This was the first purpose built cinema in Waterloo and it's 660 seats were well patronised until competition arrived in 1920 from the 'Regent' & 'Corona' followed by the 'Plaza' (Odeon) in 1939. Being in the shadow of these larger picture palaces, the 'Queens' was thus relegated to screening second-run films and 'B' movies. To illustrate the point, the billboards above lure the passer-by with 'The Marriage Symphony' starring Clive Brook & Diana Wynyard - *who?* I hear you ask. Also noteworthy are the row of shops beyond the Alexandra pub which stood opposite Waterloo railway station before demolition in the 1970's.

(right) As Linacre Road doesn't begin until the Bootle & Litherland border is reached by the 'Pacific Hotel' much further on, this view is wrongly captioned and should have been titled Stanley Road with a Bootle series number. That said, it was taken in March 1935 at the cross-roads of Knowsley Road (left) and Linacre Lane (right). Often referred to as the 'three banks' roundabout, note the curved swathe through same to allow the easy passage of trams and the veil of tram-wires necessary to serve such a junction. Part of the 'Broadway' cinema can be seen beyond the bank on the left - although destroyed by enemy action in the May blitz, the site came to be occupied by the 'Gaumont' (later 'Odeon') picture-house in 1956.

LINACRE ROAD, LITHERLAND.   L.S.12.

OXFORD ROAD, WATERLOO.   W.11.

(left) Looking north along Oxford Road, Waterloo on 18th March 1935 at it's junction with Sanheys Avenue. Denton's stationers is on the corner with Delve's cycles, Taylor's grocery, Davies fish & chip shop, Withey's bootmakers and Read's grocers & bakery beyond. Note the bill-board by Denton's door publicising the 'Regent' cinema's attractions - the display of such posters usually earning the proprietor free tickets.

KNOWSLEY ROAD, BOOTLE.

B.5.

Anyone having this card will be puzzled why more subject matter appears here than on their copy. The reason is that the above was printed from the whole 6½" x 4¾" negative as opposed to the 5½" x 3½" cards which were 'contact' printed from same. As a result, much beyond the caption area was omitted from the published item - a common practise amongst photographers of the day. This view includes the 'Gainsborough' cinema and was taken on 20th March 1935 as were all of Feilden's Bootle subjects. The film showing that day was *College Rhythm*, a 1934 semi-musical starring no-one of note which Halliwell records as having left nothing to posterity. The cinema opened in 1922, closed in 1960 and spent longer as a Bingo Hall before being demolished in 2003.

W. T. WRIGHT

William Thomas Wright, born 1845, was to Bootle what Stephen Cushing was to Crosby - a passionate and prolific photographer. A founder member and officer of the Bootle Photographic Society, he was active from at least 1884 until a few years before his death in 1912. Although not known for certain, the date he assumed professional status is thought to have been around 1890. His trademark was simply 'W & Co.' and these initials are usually to be found in small letters on the obverse of his postcards.

A devout Christian, he was also involved with the Ash Street Mission, the Linacre bible class and eventually became Superintendent of the local Sunday School. His substantial obituary in the August 26th edition of the Bootle Times recalls *'.....he brought a warm-hearted enthusiasm and devoted spirit into all the religious work he undertook, and his genial personality and high character won him a large circle of friends..........'* These fine sentiments were supported by a large and impressive list of mourners.

His home address was 26 Ash Street, Bootle but the business premises at 324 Stanley Road was often cited and it is likely he had rooms above there also. This latter building, three doors away from the 'Bootle Metropole' theatre, was occupied by other members of his family who curiously seem to have traded chamois leather products and photographic supplies from the same building. If that wasn't diverse enough, a brother, A. Wright, ran a haulage business - see the photo opposite.

Failing health from 1909 forced William to curtail much of his activities but his photographic legacy is thought to have been carried on by

family members until about 1917, beyond which the Stanley Road address is only listed in directories as 'Wright & Co - leather cutters'.

With no records having been traced, it must be assumed that the negatives have long been dispersed, lost or destroyed and the absence of any reference numbers forces collectors of these cards to guess at the size of the portfolio.

At the time of writing, 132 cards have been noted (for the Merseyside area) but what percentage of the whole this represents is difficult to assess - with half of William Wright's career spent prior to the picture postcard boom, he is unlikely to have produced a large number of cards prior to 1900. His passion for the subject would have compensated in later times as there is evidence

of this in the number of winter scenes he took - unlike many of his contemporaries, William Wright appears to have been active throughout the year. If Cushing averaged a hundred views per annum, it is therefore reasonable to assume that the W.& Co. output was 50% greater and this pushes the grand total towards 2000 with the addition of his early exposures and the post-1912 views.

Aside from his Sefton, Liverpool, Wirral and shipping subjects, he occasionally took photos as far afield as North Wales and Scotland and not merely for leisure purposes - these were also marketed as postcards. It should be noted that only his Sefton subjects are tabulated in this volume - his other work in the region will feature in future volumes.

At this point, mention should be made of Southport. Although now in the Sefton area, it was never intended to include it in this series as, like many resorts, it had a busy and specialist postcard industry of it's own. It is curious, therefore, that prolific photographers like Cushing and Wright don't seem to have exploited such a rich vein of trade - the nearest either appear to have ventured was Freshfield. It is possible they were sub-contracted for such work by Valentine and clauses prevented them from selling their own cards in that area. Although neither name appear in the registers, this is not uncommon if the local agent supervised the commission (see 'Dove's Library' caption on page 70). In support of the exclusion theory, Wright also appears to have avoided New Brighton.

Sadly, many of these narrow-bordered sepia cards suffer from fading or fingerprint ghosting and this usually indicates they were not 'fixed' sufficiently or handled with care - a talented photographer he most certainly was but haste in the darkroom unwittingly flawed an otherwise impeccable archive. (biography and inset courtesy of Peter Woolley) (right) A branch of the Wright family empire was the haulage business of Elm Street, Bootle and this circa 1915 posed view shows their Clayton & Shuttleworth 5 ton steam wagon, registration no. FE 1878. Other W & Co. cards exist showing this vehicle with crude side panels containing loads of up to 35 children on the occasion of Church outings. Not having the usual 'W & Co.' title on the front, this card is one of a minority which had a printed identity on the reverse - *'Wright & Co. "Real Photo" Bootle, Lancs.'*

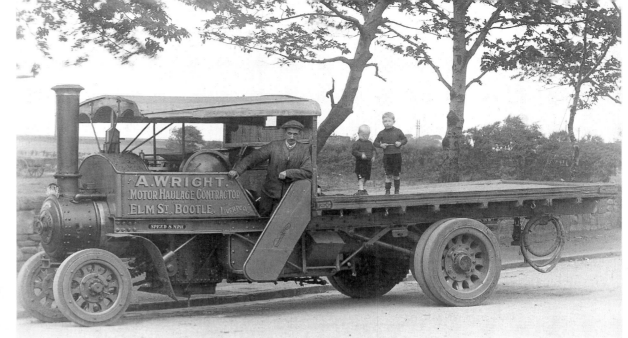

(left) Cushing and Wright's active periods overlapped by five years or more and they often invaded each other's area. This view of Liverpool Road, Crosby, looking towards Moor Lane was taken by William Wright around 1906 and shows a horse-drawn dray outside the 'Crosby Vaults' pub on the left - this building became a cafe around 1926 before being converted into shops (see pages 16 & 34 also). Unlike many contemporaries, winter scenes feature regularly among Wright's cards and give an indication of his prowess with a camera - the presence of snow frequently causing photographers to miscalculate the exposure.

 (upper) A circa 1906 'W. & Co.' view of the entrance to Seaforth Barracks on Claremont Road. The two posters on the left are aimed at persuading men to 'take the King's shilling' - one is headed *Recruits wanted for the Militia* whilst the other illustrates *Tunics of the British Army*. Built in 1882, this large establishment between Rawson and Sandy Roads was the home of some famous regiments down the years including the Kings Royal Dragoons, the Royal Field Artillery and the Royal Scots Greys. Troops from here manned the Seaforth Battery and rioting took place outside these very gates in 1914 when relatives tried to see loved ones about to be sent overseas. Closed in 1958 when the Liverpool Kings Regiment was amalgamated with the Manchester Regiment, the site has since been redeveloped as housing including two large tower blocks - see map on page 41.

 (lower) From beauty spot to 'Black Spot' - compare this view of Moor Lane, Ince Woods, with the busy thoroughfare it has since become. The cobbled leafy lane with it's occasional horse-drawn vehicle is now a high speed section of the A565 Liverpool to Southport road - noted for it's accidents, even fleet-footed squirrels require specially erected rope 'crossings'. Franked 14th September 1904, the message on the reverse of this W & Co. card ably corroborates the point raised in paragraph 3 of the Introduction - *'Dear Moll, Will not be able to go to Arcadia tonight. Will you see Jessie at eight just as arranged please. Yours etc., Kitty'*. Sent from Seaforth to Jubilee Drive in Liverpool, Moll would have received it within hours courtesy of a half-penny stamp and the highly efficient postal system.

W & CO (WRIGHT & CO)

 (above) A view of Stanley Road, Bootle looking north from the canal bridge around 1905. With the whole of the left-hand vista having long been redeveloped into the New Strand shopping centre, nothing on this W & Co. card is as it is today. The shops nearest the camera include Piercy's Ironmongers with a wonderful array of hardware including a mangle. Just beyond, an alley and steps led to Carolina Street which gave access to canal wharves, warehouses, mills and rows of terraced streets nick-named 'Little America' - see opposite.

 (opposite page) Apart from pockets of surviving terraced housing here and there, this 1906 map of Strand Road, Bootle is unrecognisable today. Even the railway station was different with platforms serving 4 tracks and access from both ends - hence it's name at the time, 'Marsh Lane & Strand Road'.

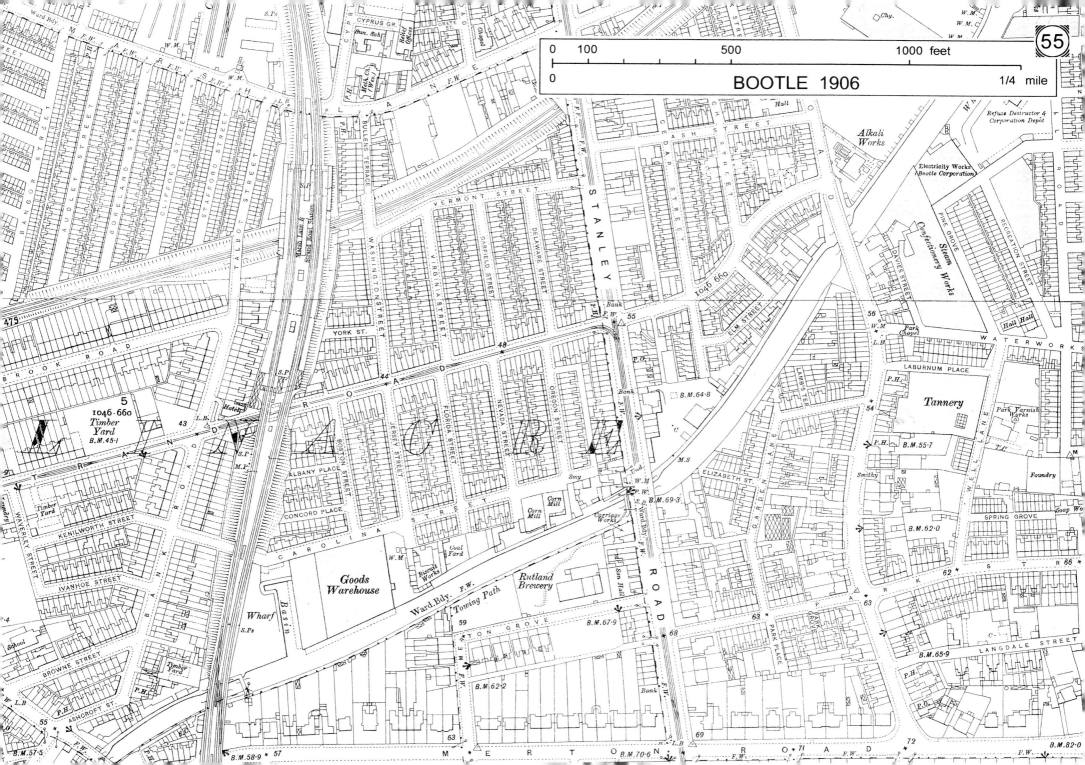

BOOTLE 1906

55

0 100   500   1000 feet

0   1/4 mile

(left) A Wright & Co. card recording members of the local fire brigade with their themed float for a Bootle Carnival in the Edwardian period. Not only an offensive but punishable act today, it must be stressed that this was a hundred years ago in the days before racial integration and few minorities would have been present to witness the deed, least of all be offended by it. By no means uncommon in that era, behaviour of this kind was a tactless bi-product of those colonial times yet considered little more than harmless fun. With the canal left, this photograph was posed at the refuse destructor wharf near Pine Grove which was usually the rallying point for such parades - note the walled ramp to the right.

(right) Malta Road and the Welsh Chapel at the corner of Marsh Lane in Bootle as captured by William Wright at an unknown date other than some time during the Edwardian era. Surviving into the 1970's, this and the small group of streets surrounding it were bulldozed in favour of Washington Parade and the extension of North Park to Marsh Lane.

(opposite page) The significant features of this 1906 portion of Bootle are sections of Knowsley Road as yet unbuilt and the dominating nature of Marsh Lane railway junction. Whilst still maintained as a single track strategic link to Aintree, a regular electrified service from there to Liverpool Exchange operated via this junction between 1906 and 1951. Note also the original layout of housing around Chesnut Grove (north of St. James R.C. church).

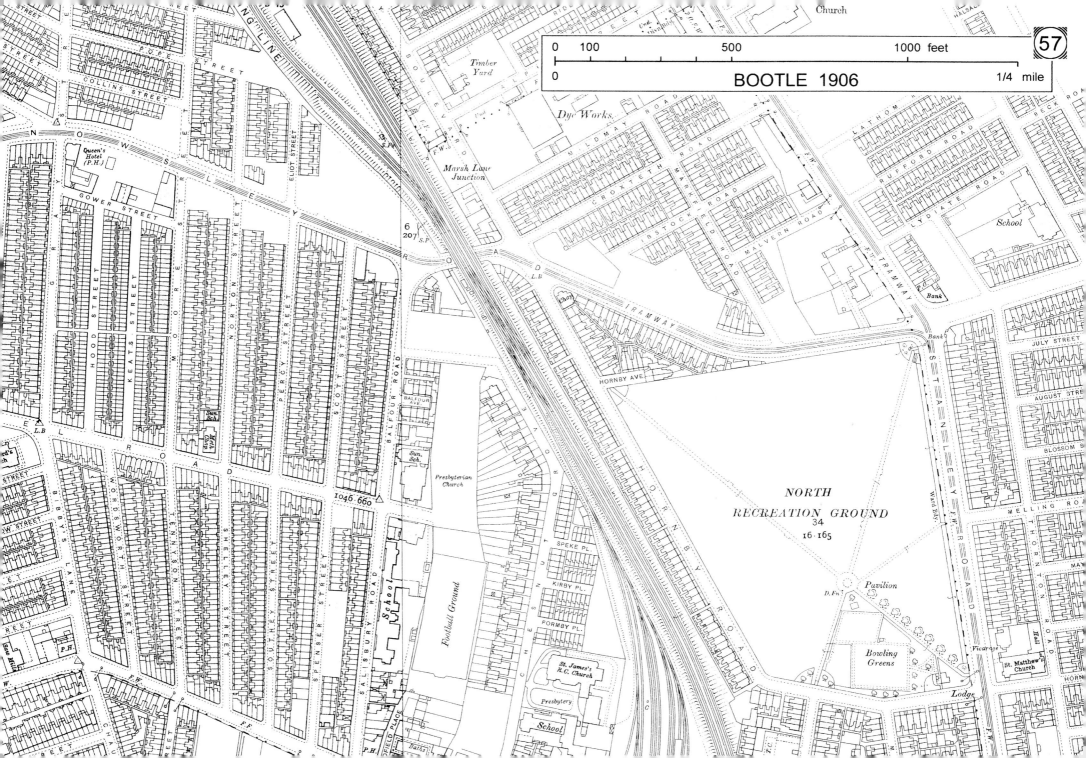

BOOTLE 1906

0 100   500   1000 feet
0   1/4 mile

Church

Timber
Yard

Dye Works

Marsh Lane
Junction

NORTH
RECREATION GROUND
34
16·165

Pavilion

Bowling
Greens

Football Ground

Presbyterian
Church

St. James's
R.C. Church

Presbytery

School

St. Matthew's
Church

Lodge

Vicarage

Hall

Queen's
Hotel
(P.H.)

Speke Pl.

Kirby Pl.

Formby Pl.

Hornby Ave.

Balfour Ave.

School

School

Baths

Stew Mill

1046·660

6
207

Bank

Bank

P.O.
Bank

TRAMWAY

TRAMWAY

(right) This view of an old smithy at Formby is thought to be the one off Church Road near to the junction with Cable Street - see map on page 27. Captured by William Wright at a time when horse power meant that literally, the blacksmith was an integral part of the community and the 'Mr. Fixit' of his day. He was kept busy with all manner of metal-forging, shoeing and repairs - a wagon axle appears to be receiving attention here as the nearby cartwheel and hub suggest. Note the posters displayed which include one for the Southport Visiter and another giving details of the 1871 Dogs Act.

(left) Taken in Edwardian days when Formby was recognisably more rural, this W. & Co. view of Cross Green was taken from the corner of Three Tuns Lane and Duke Street. The 'Blundell Arms' hotel is left, the village green with it's cross central and Liverpool Road can be seen disappearing into the distance beyond the group who appear to be observing the Sabbath.

(opposite page) Drawn prior to the population explosion in Formby, this survey of 1906 clearly defines the area around Chapel Lane as the hub of village life. Compare this with the map of today to see how much greenery has given way to the myriad of Crescents, Ways and Closes that exist now.

FORMBY 1906

(left) Railway stations have long been popular subjects for postcard photographers and this is Wright's view of Formby around 1910. The subject allowed use of the pun *'just a few lines from.......'* by both sender and publisher - the latter often using the phrase in the view's caption. Looking in the direction of Liverpool, this was taken before the road bridge replaced the level crossing and footbridge. Note also the boards instructing passengers where to stand for their preferred compartment - first or third class and smoking or non-smoking. Whilst being forgiven for thinking this was merely in keeping with the courtesy of those times, it should be remembered that the prompt boarding of passengers was in everyone's interest. With trains every ten minutes and fifteen intermediate stations between Liverpool & Southport, time wasted at each could disrupt schedules and especially during peak periods when expresses also operated.

(right) School Lane, Formby is the subject of this 'W.& Co.' issue some time prior to 1906. Halsall Lane is to the left of the three shops which at that time were Thomas Slater's grocers, Evans' fancy goods & stationery and George Clarke's Ironmongers - note the diverse array of goods outside the latter with trellis-work, flower-pots, basket-ware and deck-chairs evident. Evans' was soon to become the second shop of Stephen Cushing who ran it until 1909 but it became Frederick Derbyshire's stationers from about 1911. Following much redevelopment, the block no longer exists in this form.

(upper) Callous though it was, disasters spelled good business as far as postcard publishers were concerned and many would rush to get their photographs in the shops ahead of the competition. With newspapers the only media at that time and not being noted for the picture content nor quality we expect today, a good photograph of a newsworthy incident could sell many hundreds of copies over a wide area. In order to boost sales further, captions accompanying them were usually expanded to explain the incident and this is the case here with this W. & Co. record of the Hall Road disaster of 27th July 1905 - *'standing train shewing wheels of wrecked car driven underneath'*. Sets of up to twelve variations were often produced but these are usually identified by numbers in brackets (i.e.) *Hall Road Disaster (1)* etc. Twenty one people lost their lives and a further 45 were injured in this tragedy when a Southport bound express hit an empty train.

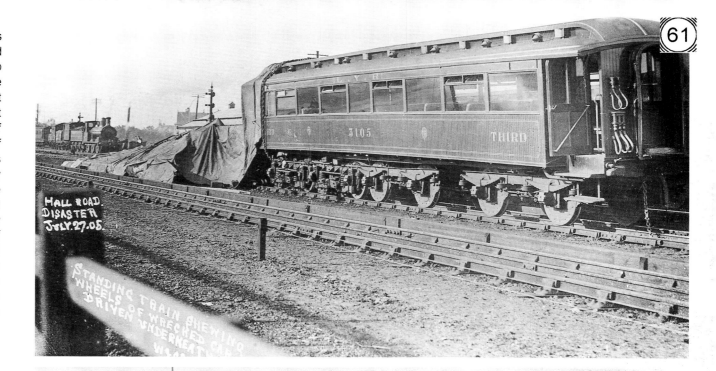

(lower) Waterloo Town Hall in Edwardian days as photographed by Wright from the junction of Great Georges Road and Church Road. The latter is on the right and part of Thorougood's 'Lion Brewery' which stood on Queen Street can be seen in the distance. Apart from detail differences, much of the Town Hall is unchanged but the brewery has long disappeared - see page 69 also.

(above & left)   These two 'W.& Co.' cards show Bootle's Oriel Road from both directions and were possibly taken the same day some time around 1906. Above, the canopied forecourt of Oriel Road station is visible on the left with the 'Windham Hotel' opposite at the junction of St.Edmonds Road. The shops to the right of the pub are (left to right) Wright's confectioners, Houghton's drapers, Hall & Co. coal merchants, Green's tobacconists and Swinton's chemists. The latter, behind the ornate lamp, had previously been post-office to the area before the large one at the corner of Balliol Road was built - the words 'Post Office' being just visible in the lead light wording above it's windows. Despite the passing of a hundred years, the pub is still trading but all bar one of the shops has been converted to dwellings.

The left hand view shows the other side of the pub from St.Catherines Road (Nos.15 to 41). The houses at the far end survive as flats but the site of the first seven (Nos.15 to 27) is now occupied by a modern apartment block. Directories for the period reveal that the professional classes lived here with 3 merchants, a doctor and 4 engineers in their number.

(above)   This postcard of 'Bootle Village' or to be more precise, the part of Litherland Road which junctions Merton Road, is a well known W. & Co. issue but copies are usually heavily faded which ruins full appreciation of the background detail - fortunately, this example is only slightly affected and is worthy of full page enlargement. Although postally used in 1906, others exist that were franked a year earlier - the message on the reverse informs us that the young lady dressed in white in the centre of the view is a Miss B. Randall of 2 Litherland Road which is the house behind the tree on the right. Right to left from Miss Randall's home are the Post Office, Stationers (& Circulating Library) at No.4, Turpin's butchers (No.6), Lunt's bakery (No.8), Beckitt's bootmakers (No.10) and the 'Jawbone Tavern' public house at No.12. The shops being open and the presence of children suggests this photograph was taken on a Saturday.

OTHER PUBLISHERS

UNIDENTIFIED PUBLISHERS - un-numbered.

~   *1916 C 19 BRIGHTON ROAD, WATERLOO (Rimmer's Tobacconists)*
          - see illustration page 67

~   *1935 P FORMBY LIGHTHOUSE - see illustration right*

~   1910   HORNBY BOULEVARD (crowd after matchworks fire)

~   *1910 C IRWIN'S GROCERS, BOOTLE - see illustration page 2.*

~   *1916 C 95/97 LIVERPOOL ROAD, CROSBY (Henderson's &*
          Merrick's) - see illustration page 80.

~   *1912 C THOMSON ROAD, SEAFORTH - Wm. WOOD, Cowkeeper*
Pony & Trap with family posing outside No.4 - see illustration page 1.

~   1908   STRAND ROAD, BOOTLE (horse-drawn ambulance)
Note - This card has the hallmarks of a 'W & Co.' issue but without the usual
identification. The fact that it is a Bootle subject also supports this suspicion.

~   1911   THEATRE, STANLEY RD, BOOTLE ('Metropole' - portrait)

UNIDENTIFIED PUBLISHER

4   1935 C ORIEL ROAD (from Bootle Oriel Road Station)
7   *1935 P CROSBY ROAD NORTH, WATERLOO (Fay's Motors)*
          - see illustration opposite.
12   1930 C DERBY PARK ENTRANCE, WORCESTER RD, BOOTLE
Note - This sepia toned and bordered series probably numbered little more
than 20 or so and they resemble Valentine issues at first glance.

(right)   An extremely rare close-up of the Formby Lighthouse and
cottage from an inland viewpoint some time prior to 1935. Issued by
an unknown publisher and appearing to be missing it's top, this structure,
built in 1719, was simply of the chimney type which had their lamps visible
from one side only. Stephen Cushing did take at least one view of it (No.980)
but his landscape effort was much more distant. This light is reported to have
last seen service in 1856 but it wasn't felled until 1941, primarily to deprive
the Luftwaffe of a landmark so close to the docks.

Formby Lighthouse.

CROSBY ROAD NORTH, WATERLOO.

7

Post-marked August 1935, this view of Crosby Road North near Molyneux Road is from an unknown publisher. Despite it's professional looking caption and resemblance to a Valentine's issue, it is likely to have come from a minor source - only two cards having surfaced with the same characteristics. Notwithstanding this, it is noteworthy for it's depiction of Fay's 'Night & Day' Motor Garage which was first built in 1929. Although most of us remember it as 'Camerons' which it became shortly after this photograph was taken, the garage continued servicing motor vehicles well into the 1980's before a complete rebuild reduced it's status to filling station. It closed in this capacity in 2004 and the site has since been levelled pending redevelopment.

UNIDENTIFIED PUBLISHER

7		(No. circled) 'AQUITANIA' AT GLADSTONE DOCK
15	1910	(No. circled) MILLERS BRIDGE (St.Winefred's procession)

UNIDENTIFIED PUBLISHER

10	1926 P	CROSBY ROAD, WATERLOO - see illustration below
14		CROSBY ROAD, W/LOO (WCMS bus near St.John's Road)
17	1926 P	CROSBY ROAD, WATERLOO (WCMS bus at 5 Lamps)
57		LIVERPOOL ROAD (by Myers Road & WCMS bus)

Note - With W&CMS buses on all of these bordered regular cards, they were thought to be unmarked company 'officials' until No.57 was found - they are thus most likely the work of a local enthusiast (except N.N.Forbes of Waterloo).

UNIDENTIFIED PUBLISHER

76		DERBY PARK LAKE, BOOTLE

UNIDENTIFIED PUBLISHER

A 1		TOWN HALL, LITHERLAND
A 9		CHURCH ROAD, LITHERLAND
A 35		MERTON ROAD, BOOTLE
A 36		STRAND ROAD, BOOTLE
A 38		WAR MEMORIAL, BOOTLE
A 45		STANLEY ROAD, BOOTLE
A 48	1936 P	TRINITY ROAD, BOOTLE
A 59		THE OLD MILL, CROSBY
A 63		BRIDGE ROAD, LITHERLAND
A 64		BRIDGE ROAD, LITHERLAND
A 65		KNOWSLEY ROAD, BOOTLE
A 68	1935 P	THE SHORE, BLUNDELLSANDS
A 145	1938 P	ELM ROAD, SEAFORTH - see illustration opposite
A 147		SEAFORTH ROAD, SEAFORTH (& 'Palladium' cinema)

Note - A numerous yet charming series which remains anonymous. Although Elsie Ackland was at first suspected, these bordered cards are more likely to be the work of Dorothea Dixon, 14 Rawson Rd, for the reasons given opposite and decade concerned. Both sepia toned and regular prints have been noted.

(left) Franked September 1926, this view of Crosby Road North was taken much earlier in the year as the disused tramlines are still in situ. South Road and the 'Liver Hotel' can be seen left with the Liver Forge operated by James Stewart Roughley beyond - *'Horse Shoer and General Smith'* reads the sign. The land beyond there was then occupied by large houses with ample front gardens whose names were *The Poplars, Tacna, Norman Hurst, Ivy Dene, Eaton Bank, Spring Bank and Riada Bank*. The 'Plaza' (later 'Odeon') cinema which came to dominate the site was still fourteen years away but the latter two properties made way for shops earlier than this. The second house, 'Tacna', was long the home and studio of local photographer, Ellis Vernon Empson, who operated from 1908 to 1939 and beyond.

CROSBY RD. WATERLOO. 10

(left) But for the fact that this card was postally used, the subject of this anonymous 'commission' would have remained a mystery for many years more. Sent to an address in Hightown, the message hinted the sender was not too distant but when their name was seen to co-incide with the one above the shop doorway, it was simply a matter of checking the local directory to see that there was a Rimmer's tobacconist and newsagent at 19 Brighton Road, Waterloo. As to a date more accurate than WW1, although the postmark was missing, the 'News of the World' placard provided a vital clue - with Sunday, June 11th just visible, this had to make it 1916. The last piece of the jig-saw pointed to Stephen Cushing - the 'Post Card' backing is of a style and type frequently used by the prolific publisher from Crosby.

(right) Elm Road, Seaforth from the charming but anonymous series which appear to cover South Sefton. Judging by surviving issues, the publisher seems to have been based in Bootle or Litherland in the mid 30's and scrutiny of the lists on pages 4 & 5 suggests two candidates - Robertson of 76 Bridge Road, Litherland (1929-1939) and Dixon of 14 Rawson Road, Seaforth (1932-1935). The latter was an ex-city centre based photographer and curiously enough, this view shows Rawson Road in the distance near the very block where Miss Dixon lived - given the minor nature of this road, can this be dismissed as pure coincidence? Mummery's bakery at No.24 Elm Road is opposite the Congregational church - both fell victim to the WW2 blitz.

UNIDENTIFIED PUBLISHER

BR 26   1921 P   MARINE TERRACE, WATERLOO
BR 49   GREAT GEORGES ROAD, WATERLOO

AEROFILMS LTD. - Hendon, London, NW8
AIRCO AERIALS - 15 Furnival St, London

Both issued aerial cards of Gladstone Dock in the 1920's but refer to the special feature on Aerial PC Publishers in the Liverpool South & City volume.

ALLEN & SONS - Herbert Allen & Sons, Postcard
Publishers, 59/61 Warbreck Rd, Blackpool (circa 1922)
later 75 Talbot Road, Blackpool (circa 1928 & beyond 1934)

868   1925 C   STANLEY ROAD, BOOTLE
Note - With a wide white border and floral relief (often called 'deckled edge'), these sepia tinted cards are identical to those of 'A.J.Evans' and undoubtedly came from the same printer - see Liverpool North volume for A.J.Evans.

BARTONS SERIES - Wm.Barton, 15 Cable St. L/Pool

~   1913 P   ALEXANDRA PARK (Crosby)

BELL'S SERIES - Bells Photo Co., Leigh on Sea, Essex

25994   1908 P   SOUTH ROAD, WATERLOO

DOVE'S LIBRARY - John Samuel Dove, 127 South Rd
& 151 St.Johns Rd, Waterloo (both c.1905) then 105 South Rd
(c.1914 to 1939 and beyond) - see biography below.

~		ADELAIDE GARDENS, WATERLOO
~	1920	THE FRONT, BLUNDELLSANDS (New Brighton Tower)
~	1916 P	RIVER VIEW, BLUNDELLSANDS
~	1916 P	CARNEGIE LIBRARY, WATERLOO
~	1908 P	MERTON ROAD (marked 'T.Dove' - brother Tom Dove**)
~		ST.JOSEPHS CHURCH, BLUNDELLSANDS
~	1908	STANLEY RD BY MELLING RD (**) (temperance march)
~	1906 P	STRAND ROAD (Bootle Fire Brigade) (**)
~	1918 C	*WATERLOO AERIAL (1) (Beach Lawn) - see illus. page 70.*
~	1918 C	*WATERLOO AERIAL (2) (South Road) - see illus. opposite.*
~	1918 C	WATERLOO AERIAL (3) (Cambridge Road)
V11		SEAFORTH SANDS STATION (**)

Note - A grandson states there were never more than 20 postcards published by Dove's Library as it was preferred to market those of others such as Stephen Cushing of Crosby. Most of those that were issued have crude captioning.

John Samuel Dove, born 1873, took his first photos of soldiers en route to the Boer War - he was employed as a ship's barber and paid ½d per chin ! The plates were processed by his brother Tom (also a barber, as were 2 other brothers) who sold prints to the subjects relatives. John returned to Liverpool by 1895 and continued as a barber before opening stationery premises at 127 South Road and 151 St.John's Road, Waterloo, around 1905. Both were given up in favour of another stationers at 105 South Road circa 1914.

John befriended Henry Melly (the renowned early aviator who ran a flying school on Waterloo beach from circa 1911) and took at least three aerial views of the area as his passenger in 1913 or 1914 (see examples on pages 69 & 70). They are no later than this as Melly was forced to abandon flying shortly afterwards owing to war restrictions. John's son, also named John Samuel, was born in 1902 and...(continued opposite)

Mr H. MELLY AT WATERLOO

(left)   Henry Melly on Waterloo Sands with one of his early flying machines - in view of their association, this anonymous card of 1911 was quite possibly published by John Samuel Dove (see text).

BIRDSEYE VIEW OF WATERLOO TAKEN FROM R.A.F. AEROPLANE

(continued)..although initially pursuing the careers of marine engineer and professional golfer, entered the business around 1928 and expanded the circulating library stock to accommodate 30 outlets. Note that John senior's brother, Tom, contributed four or more views for postcards. John senior also undertook at least four 'commissions' for Valentine & Co. from 1932 - see page 70. He died in 1952 but the business continued under John Samuel (II) until retirement in 1971 - he died in 1985. See also aerial photography feature in the Liverpool South & City volume. (courtesy of John Stuart Dove & Russell Dove).

(above) Taken by John Samuel Dove senior aboard Henry Melly's aeroplane circa 1914 (see text). The Queen's Cinema on South Road is visible (opened 1913) as are Dean, Wesley, Chapel and Queen Streets, most of which were cleared for the erection of two tower blocks. Other absentees today include the Wesleyan Church and School (middle) and Lion Brewery (top right) - the latter was built in 1877 and served the 'Thorougood' pub chain which included the nearby Queens Hotel & Boar's Head in Crosby. Acquired by Threlfall's in 1921, the company's claim of 'Noted Ales' was a valid one - surviving documents reveal that the House of Lords Refreshment Rooms was a regular patron.

(above) Another aerial view taken by John Samuel Dove (assisted by Henry Melly) with Beach Lawn and Adelaide Terrace running left to right. Circa 1914, much has yet to be built as will be seen.

(left) Dove's Library is second left in this circa 1932 view of South Road which was allegedly taken by John Samuel (I) on Valentine's behalf for the princely sum of £12, copyright inclusive. Although the J.V. register attributes the view to a J.G. Scrutton, sub-contracting did take place and the latter may simply have acted as agent on this occasion. Dove is directly registered as having taken three Waterloo Shore views for them in 1939 (Nos. H 2721 to 23).

SOUTH ROAD, WATERLOO.

223292 J

EMPSON E V - Ellis Vernon Empson, 18 Kinross Road, Waterloo (1908-1910) 'Tacna' Crosby Road North, Waterloo (1910-1939) and 2 South Road, Waterloo (1924-1925) - Sandringham Series.

~   1908   OPENING NEW LIBRARY (Waterloo)

HARTLEY BROS. - 2 South Rd, W/loo (1900-1912)

~   1903   WATERLOO STATION DISASTER

(left) John 'Cockle' Johnson as photographed for the Hulme series around 1907. Said to have been noted for his cleanliness, this close-up suggests his clothing fell somewhat short of the mark - but, it must be remembered that standards differed then - see below also.

H.S. - Uncertain origin but most likely an abbreviation for the 'Hulme Series' (prior to or later than) - see below.

HS 18		BLUNDELLSANDS SHORE
HS 19	1908 P	BLUNDELLSANDS COTTAGE HOME
HS 21	1908 P	ADELAIDE TERRACE, WATERLOO
HS 56	1907 P	LITTLE CROSBY CHURCH

HULME SERIES - J.Hulme, photographer, Mersey Road, Blundellsands (1907-1910)

~		AGNES ROAD, BLUNDELLSANDS
~	1907 P	BLUNDELLSANDS ROAD EAST
~		THE CHANNEL FLEET, BLUNDELLSANDS SHORE
~		WAITING FOR CHANNEL FLEET, BLUNDELLSANDS
~		WATCHING THE CHANNEL FLEET, B/SANDS SHORE
~		COAST GUARDS, BLUNDELLSANDS (Naval Militia)
~	1907 C	COOKS ROAD, CROSBY (from Victoria Road)
~		CROSBY FIRE BRIGADE (protest demonstration)
~	1907 P	JOHN JOHNSON (portrait format) - see illustration left.
~		LAND MARK BLOWN DOWN (shore)
~		MAY DAY PROCESSION, CROSBY (Fire Brigade)
~		ST.LUKES, CROSBY
~		THE OLD VILLAGE, CROSBY (Liverpool Road)
~		ELECTRIC TRAIN AT WATERLOO (from Walmer Road)

Note - cards in this bordered series have the caption and origin printed on the front in a faded white type-written form as seen in the example on the left. Regular, sepia-tinted and mild sepia tones all noted.

(lower left)   John Johnson had as many nick-names as facets to his personality - 'Jack' Johnson, 'Cockle' Johnson, 'Hermit of the Shore' and 'Roast Beef', the latter referring to his weather-beaten complexion. Said to have been wounded at the battle of Alma in the Crimea and later shipwrecked from New Orleans to Liverpool, no wonder he turned to the safer pursuits of gamekeeping, beachcombing and cockling. 'Alt Cottage', as this ramshackle hut was known, was built near Hall Road in 1871 because of his wish to live near his work. With only a cat and dog for company, he allegedly lived there for 50 years but his eventual fate has not been traced. Reportedly 79 years old in 1907 and enjoying 'uncommon rude health', this presumes he reached 90-plus before departing. In light of such notoriety, it is both sad and curious that his passing appears to have gone unreported - unless he was forced to move inland as a result of the coastal erosion? (Cushing card No.1468 of circa 1907).

J. J. - John Johnston, photographer, of 33 Eleanor Rd, Litherland (C1904 to C1905) OR Joseph Jardalla, Stationer, of 7 Litherland Rd, Bootle (C1900 to C1903).

JJ	1904	FIELD LANE, LITHERLAND
JJ	*1904*	*LITHERLAND BRIDGE (& 'Red Lion' pub) - see illus. below*

KNOTT W - nothing known of this publisher.

~		CROSBY FIRE BRIGADE
H 10	1908 P	HIGHTOWN (Windermere Road)

LILYWHITE LTD. - Halifax, Yorkshire (c.1910 - 1939)

LPL 17	1922 P	GLADSTONE DOCK

McCABE J - Joseph McCabe, stationer & tobacconist, 96 Seaforth Road, Seaforth (1900-1930C).

~		ST. JAMES CHURCH, BOOTLE

Note - There was some form of connection between McCabe and W & Co. and is thought to have been a distribution or production agreement.

MERSEY DOCKS & HARBOUR BOARD

~	1919 C	GLADSTONE DOCKS (aerial view)
~	1935 C	GLADSTONE BRANCH DOCK No.1.
~	*1935 C*	*ROUGH CARGO BERTH, CARRIERS DOCK - see ill. opposite*

Note - There were two series of sepia cards from this company at least a decade apart - the earlier one being taken by Aerofilms. 'Port of Liverpool' is common to most but all bear the circular company seal on the back - see other volumes also.

O.N.S. - nothing known of this publisher.

~	1914 C	AQUITANIA AT GLADSTONE GRAVING DOCK
~	1914 C	AQUITANIA PASSING WATERLOO (from beach)
~	1914	SHORE FIELD, CROSBY RD (A.S.C. troops camped)
~	1914	SHORE FIELD, CROSBY RD (tents close-up
~	1914	SHORE FIELD, CROSBY RD (preparing dinner)
~	1914	SHORE FIELD, CROSBY RD (men spud-bashing)
~	1914	SHORE FIELD, CROSBY RD (field attack drill)
~	1914	SHORE FIELD, CROSBY RD (fife & drum march)
~	1914	SHORE FIELD, CROSBY RD (lorry close-up)
~	1914 C	SEAFORTH ROAD, OLD VILLAGE
~	1914 C	S.S. SCHOOL PLAYING TENNIS AT SEAFORTH REC.
~	*1916 P*	*WOODLAND ROAD, SEAFORTH - see illustration opposite*

Note - This publisher operated within a small area and probably from home for a short time in 1914. Despite a search of the 1913 directory, the initials do not match any householders in the area so he (or she) was most likely a junior member of the family and with no known material beyond 1914, could also have fallen victim to the First World War. All known cards have crude captions.

(left) This card of 1904 captures the original 'Red Lion Inn' more accurately than the canal bridge beyond. Unless depicting a particular event, it is unusual for cards to be dated yet we can be certain the figure refers to the year as two cards have been traced bearing same. As the above listing alludes to, who 'J.J.' was is open to debate. My guess would be Johnston as he is known to have been a photographer, albeit a novice judging by the quality. Although certain stationers did publish their own cards, the directories record that Jardalla had vacated the area by 1904. The larger present-day 'Red Lion' replaced the Inn not long afterwards - see page 32 also.

Litherland J.J Bridge 1904

(left) Postcards with inked crosses on the front are fairly common but annoying to collectors as they often deface or devalue them. Usually done to illustrate a message on the reverse, the marks on this card are no exception ....*'this road is where we live and the cross at the end of the street is the sea. The cross on the house is where we lodge. If we look out of the sitting room window we can see the sea.'*....... Posted at 10.15am on 25th April, 1916, this photograph was almost certainly taken a couple of years earlier - see publisher's note opposite under O.N.S.

WOODLAND-RD

Seaforth O.N.S.

PORT OF LIVERPOOL

ROUGH CARGO BERTH, CARRIERS DOCK

(right) A Mersey Docks and Harbour Board view which is self-explanatory other than it was one of the second series of cards which were issued by the company in the mid-thirties. The building in the distance is the Liverpool branch of Harland & Wolff, ship and engine repairers, which stood on Regent Road, Bootle, south of Howe Street.

PARTOON A W - Arthur W Partoon, 2 South Road, Waterloo (1912-1924)

~		MERCHANT TAYLORS GIRLS SCHOOL, GR.CROSBY
~		NEW BRIGHTON (& Tower from Waterloo)
~	1870 C	1st ST.NICHOLAS CHURCH (Mersey Rd - published C1915)
~	1914 P	PARK ROAD, WATERLOO
~		THE SHORE, WATERLOO
~	*1915 P*	*SOUTH ROAD / ALBERT ROAD, WATERLOO - see ill. below*
~		SOUTH ROAD / LORNE ROAD, WATERLOO
~	1916	SOUTH ROAD (Military procession 6th July)

Note : A series of mildly tinted sepia cards with a narrow border.

RIDGWAY T J - Thomas J Ridgway, 103 Stanley Road, Bootle (1926-1938)

34	1926 P	BOOTLE MAY DAY (shire horses)
TR 3	1930	BOOTLE MAY DAY QUEEN, 1930
TR 5	1927	KINGS VISIT, JULY 1927 (dignitaries)
TR 8	1928	ST.JOAN'S PAGEANT (parade)
TR 9	1936	BOOTLE MAY DAY, 1936
TR 17	1927	KINGS VISIT, JULY 1927 (soldiers)
TR 17	1929 P	SEAFORTH STREET, BOOTLE

(below) This Partoon card of South Road, Waterloo shows their own studios above shops at the junction with Bath Street on the left. Post-marked 1915, 'Successor to Hartley Bros. Photographers' can also be read above the amply illuminated premises.

SOUTH ROAD, WATERLOO.

TR 19	1932	BOOTLE MAY DAY, 1932 (children in procession)
TR 28	1927	ANKLE COMPETITION, BOOTLE MAY DAY, 1927
TR 29	1924	BOOTLE MAY DAY, 1924 (fancy dress)

Note - Ridgway had a preference for ceremony as the majority of the cards testify to but each year's work seems to have re-started at TR1 which explains duplicate numbers and conflicting dates. At least four of these regular, bordered cards bear the rubber-stamping 'Published by F.G.Thomas, 5 Lord St, Liverpool' on the rear - see later volumes for examples from other areas.

ROSEVERE B - Miss B. Rosevere, 6 Bowden Street, Litherland (circa 1921) - identity stamped on reverse of card.

~	1921	PRINCE OF WALES VISIT (Johnson's Dyeworks 5-7-1921)

SALMON SERIES - J. Salmon Ltd., Sevenoaks, Kent

7277		ALEXANDRA PARK, CROSBY
7278	1932 P	GARDEN OF REMEMBRANCE, GREAT CROSBY

S.E.H. - nothing known of this publisher.

~	1932 P	MARY ROAD, ORRELL

SMITH W H - see feature opposite

S.R. - almost certainly Sutcliffe & Ridgway of 389 Stanley Rd, Bootle (1922-1923)

6	1923	ARMISTICE DAY, BOOTLE
12	1923	ARMISTICE DAY, BOOTLE (procession)

STATE SERIES - State Publishing Company., Central Chambers, 17A South Castle St., Liverpool (c1904-1939)

2153		ALEXANDRA HALL, CROSBY

SUTCLIFFE P - Percival Sutcliffe, 457 Hawthorne Rd, (1920-1929) & 86 Knowsley Rd, Bootle (1925-1929).

~		FUNERAL OF BOOTLE'S FIRE CHIEF

VALENTINE J & CO.LTD. - see feature on page 78

WALKER J & CO.LTD. - Warwick Ln., London, E.C.

25996	1905 P	SOUTH ROAD, WATERLOO (near Curzon Road)

W. H. SMITH & SON

The origins of this famous company go back to 1790 when Henry Walton Smith ran a wholesale news delivery service from Little Grosvenor Street in London's West End. Business was slow to expand initially but by 1820 two retail shops had been acquired in the capital. Thereafter, growth was confined to the wholesale side of the business but a major leap forward came in 1848 when contracts were acquired to run bookstalls on stations of the London & North Western and Midland Railway companies.

Others like the Great Western Railway followed and by 1900 there were 1,250 WHS bookstalls at stations where one could profitably be run - this was a far greater number of outlets than any other multiple retailer at that time. Shops, however, were few and the company's reliance on stations for most of it's trade was used as a lever to extract ever higher rents when railway contracts came to be renewed.

To redress the dilemma, the company hastened it's acquisition of high street stores but the loss of the LNWR & GWR contracts in 1905 proved to be the watershed - faced with losing a fifth of their trade, the partners had little choice but to

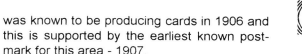

intensify the programme if decades of goodwill in those areas were not to be lost also.

A huge increase in shop premises followed and by the end of the year another 144 had been added - the majority in Wales and the western half of England. The remainder of the century saw W.H.Smith's grow to 529 stores plus 187 branches at stations and airports throughout the UK together with hundreds of outlets abroad.

Whilst the desired archive of the 'picture postcard' department has not survived, it is likely that the 1905 crisis gave birth to same. The company was known to be producing cards in 1906 and this is supported by the earliest known postmark for this area - 1907.

The 'Dale' and 'Mersey' series were dedicated to the area but small by comparison to the 'Kingsway' portfolio which covered most of the British Isles. The latter was reported as having around 6,500 subjects in 1909 and were described as 'real photographic penny cards' - 5,000 being taken by their own photographers. Stations, Trains and Ships featured heavily in the 'Kingsway' cards but the bulk of the series was topographic. Publishing rights are also

(right) Although captured in December 1947, this W.H.Smith station bookstall at Liverpool Exchange would have changed little since earlier days. Note the postcards to the right of the servery - close scrutiny reveals views of Georges Hall, Liver Buildings and the Landing Stage. Magazines in evidence include the Illustrated London News, Tatler, Punch, Holly Leaves, John Bull, Illustrated, Woman's Own and Radio Times.
(courtesy of W.H.Smith Archive Ltd.)

known to have been bought from Aerofilms, The Locomotive Publishing Co., Rotary, Robertson of Gourock and Holdsworth of Huddersfield.

Post-marks reveal that all three series were published concurrently and the ad hoc nature of subjects indicate there was no adhesion to any one district. No registers have survived but a 1909 article in the company journal, 'Newsbasket', records *our picture postcard catalogue contains 110 pages of publications and is published annually'* - if only one could be found, it would answer many questions. With few recorded post-marks beyond 1914, it is likely the company ceased producing 'Dale' & 'Mersey' cards around that time but the 'Kingsway' cards continued into the 1950's. Known dates in a collection of 'Kingsway' shipping cards

reveal that the 15,000 and 19,000 milestones were reached in 1921 & 1931 respectively so 23,000 probably existed by 1939.

What percentage were local is guesswork but the few survivors over a 33 year period point to it being around 200 which is less than 1%. Known Sefton cards are tabled below but note that the 'Dale' & 'Mersey' series appear to have gone no further than Bootle whilst the 'Kingsway' portfolio apparently ignores same in favour of Crosby & Waterloo - parochial groupings such as these suggest different sub-contractors.

Existing 'Dale' and 'Mersey' cards indicate there were about 200 and 420 issues respectively so the grand total of WHS subjects for this area was most likely about 850 - see future volumes also.

Company records show the turnover of post-cards as rising from £29,350 in 1914 to £164,399 in 1939. At 240 'penny' cards to the pound (later 1½d), this gives an indication of numbers sold in the respective 951 and 993 outlets. Following a trial, a 1929 campaign encouraged seaside branch managers to provide an area for patrons to sit, write and post their cards on the premises - this improved sales and fostered other trade.

All three series are sepia-tinted with numbered and titled fronts but the backs differ. One simply has 'Dale Series' with no publisher's details whilst the others read 'WHS Mersey Series' & 'Kingsway Real Photo Series' - the latter also bearing the company's WHS lozenge motif. (courtesy of W.H.Smith Archive Ltd. with thanks to Gail Collingburn and John Alsop)

W.H. SMITH (Dale Series)

57		CHRIST CHURCH, BOOTLE
60	1912 P	MORTON GARDENS, STANLEY ROAD, BOOTLE
62	1911 P	STANLEY GARDENS, BOOTLE
63	1913 P	SHELTER HOUSE, STANLEY GARDENS, BOOTLE
64		KING EDWARD VII STATUE, STANLEY GDNS, BOOTLE
65	1911 P	ELECTRIC TRAIN, BOOTLE STATION
66		TOWN HALL & FREE LIBRARY, BOOTLE
67		ORIEL ROAD & POST OFFICE, BOOTLE

W.H. SMITH (Mersey Series)

56	1912 P	TECHNICAL SCHOOLS, BOOTLE
57	1915 P	ORIEL ROAD & POST OFFICE, BOOTLE
59	1910 P	STANLEY ROAD / STRAND ROAD, BOOTLE
61	1914 P	STANLEY ROAD & EMMANUEL CHURCH, BOOTLE
62		STANLEY GARDENS, BOOTLE
65		BOOTLE ORIEL ROAD STATION (looking north)
68		HAWTHORNE ROAD, BOOTLE (north to Balliol Road)
156	1916 P	THE LAKE, DERBY PARK, BOOTLE
158	1912 P	THE BRIDGE, DERBY PARK, BOOTLE
159	1913 P	MERTON ROAD, BOOTLE
161	1910 P	BREEZE HILL, BOOTLE
162	*8-1911*	*STRAND ROAD, BOOTLE - 1915P - see illustration right*
163	*8-1911*	*STANLEY RD & 'METROPOLE' - 1911P - see illus. right*

W.H. SMITH (Kingsway Series)

S 4406	1907 P	SOUTH ROAD, WATERLOO (from Mount Pleasant)
S 4410	1909 P	MARINE CRESCENT, WATERLOO
S 4411	1911 P	WATERLOO FREE LIBRARY
S 4580		THE DELPH, LITTLE CROSBY
S 4582		WRIGHT'S PIT, VICTORIA ROAD, GREAT CROSBY
S 4583		FREE LIBRARY, GREAT CROSBY
S 4586		ST.NICHOLAS' CHURCH, BLUNDELLSANDS
S 4589	1912 P	BLUNDELLSANDS ROAD WEST

(opposite, both) Consecutively numbered cards from W. H. Smith's 'Mersey' series, almost certainly taken within minutes of each other by the same yet un-known (local?) photographer. Post-marked 1915 and 1911 respectively, it is the lower one which affords the opportunity of dating them precisely - the play advertised by the newly opened Metrolpole Theatre, 'A Woman's Past', ran for a week from Monday, 14th August 1911. The Strand Road view looks west from it's junction with Stanley Road whilst the Stanley Road photograph itself faces north and just allows a glimpse of the Wright (W & Co.) premises three doors beyond the theatre - see pages 50 to 63 inclusive.

162   STRAND ROAD, BOOTLE.

163 .   STANLEY ROAD & NEW THEATRE METROPOLE, BOOTLE.

J. VALENTINE & Co.

James Valentine (1815 - 1879) of Dundee ran a printing and stationery company and added portrait photography in 1851 which later boasted one of the largest photographic glasshouses.

The 1860's saw an expansion into landscape work and a Royal Warrant followed in 1868. Business was aimed at the middle classes upwards with everything from small prints at 6d. each to lavish albums costing fifteen guineas. Concentrating on Scottish subjects initially, it was James' sons, William and George, who ventured south of the border in 1882. Expansion plus pioneering work in large scale production saw Valentine's workforce rise to 100 by 1886.

A milestone was reached in 1897 when a decision to enter the picture postcard industry was taken - no doubt as a direct result of the Post Office allowing a message to be written on the address side of a card from June 16th that year. By 1899, business increased tenfold and trade with every part of the British Isles saw their stock images reach 60,000 by 1907.

The 'boom' years were also responsible for a decline in quality as competition led to most images being produced photo-mechanically. These printed and coloured issues were inferior to 'real photographic' cards and the latter were re-introduced in 1907 becoming the sole output by 1914. Photographers in their employ mostly worked in the summer months and processed the results during the winter. Others were sub-contracted locally as the need arose and John Samuel Dove of Waterloo was one such person who undertook such work - see pages 68 to 70. The company also retained as many as 40 artists who retouched originals to improve their appeal. (...continued overleaf)

From 1910, a price war with German producers severely affected trade and although the Great War brought this to an end, it too, hit hard. During this period, the company branched into the greetings card business to bolster profits. In 1937, a new factory on the outskirts of Dundee opened which was capable of a million 'real photo' postcards per week using machines that printed 28 cards on one sheet.

Over 500,000 views were registered between 1878 and 1966 and the percentage of Scottish, English, Irish and Welsh subjects (based upon post-1934 figures) suggests percentages of 36%, 50%, 6% and 8% respectively. Almost all were sepia-toned and bordered, especially from the 1920's onwards, but exceptions do occur.

The 1950's witnessed the gradual demise of the postcard in favour of greetings cards which became Valentine & Co.'s main output. No new 'mono' topographicals were registered beyond July 1966 and all production of same ceased after 1967. Valentine's were taken over by Waddington's in 1963, Hallmark in 1980 and it's long association with Dundee ended in 1994.

Although it's archive* has survived, listing the 2,055 local subjects taken between 1900-1939 would exceed economic space but summaries are given. Excluding Birkdale and Southport, there were 312 Sefton area Valentine postcards published during that period with a further 33 for Liverpool North, 540 for Liverpool South & City and 1,170 for the Wirral. With the company's marketing strategy geared to tourism, the few issued for Liverpool North reflects the poor sales potential in that area. 85% of the entire portfolio were of recreational sites - judge by the Sefton figures summarised opposite but nowhere is this more apparent than on the Wirral with New Brighton and other seaside venues accounting for most. Sadly, the records don't indicate which of the pre-1914 cards were only ever issued as 'coloured' or 'photo-mechanical' types.

With the exception of a few, all Valentine cards bear number and initials on the front but from 1934 numbering began again with a 'G' pre-fix for English cards and the exclusion of the 'J.V.' initials. As regards the reverse, there were different designs over the years until the two-globes logo and the 'Famous Throughout the World' legend standardised output around 1927.

The chronological nature of the registers allows the dating of most subjects to within a year or so but it must be pointed out that the years given are those when the views were recorded and not necessarily when they were taken. Also, out-of-date numbers were sometimes re-allocated. (Courtesy of *Dept. LIS, St, Andrews University, North Street, St.Andrews, Scotland, KY16 9TR where more information is available or log on to http://specialcollections.st-and.ac.uk.)

(below) One of only 17 Bootle subjects issued by Valentine for the period was No.78536 of Strand Road in 1914. Looking east to Stanley Road, everything here is now a memory.

STRAND ROAD, BOOTLE.

Valentine Postcards Registration Dates 1900 - 1939

(*) Registration Nos. for these years are approximate only.

1900	32485 - 34736	1921	84693 - 85757
1901	34737 - 36696	1922	85758 - 87533
1902	36697 - 38587	1923	87534 - 90916
1903	38588 - 41858	1924	90917 - 93924
1904	41859 - 46436	1925	93925 - 97656
1905	46437 - 52518	1926	97657 - 99999
1906	52519 - 57070	1926	200000 - 200960
1907	57071 - 60252	1927	200961 - 203804
1908	60253 - 61013	1928	203805 - 205864
1908*	61014 - 63074*	1929	205865 - 208470
1909*	63075 - 65894*	1930	208471 - 211448
1910*	65895 - 68713*	1931	211449 - 215545
1911*	68714 - 71532*	1932	215546 - 219417
1912*	71533 - 74339*	1933	219418 - 224436
1912	74340 - 74350	1934	224437 - 224649
1913	74351 - 78117	(below are English only)	
1914	78118 - 80289	1934	G1 - G2271
1915	80290 - 81248	1935	G2272 - G4378
1916	81249 - 81430	1936	G4379 - G6007
1917	81431 - 81507	1937	G6008 - G8257
1918	81508 - 81538	1938	G8258 - G9999
1919	81539 - 83204	1938	H1 - H993
1920	83205 - 84692	1939	H994 - H3043

99 of Ainsdale - taken between 1905 & 1939, the most common venues being Beach related with 54, Station Rd area (30), Liverpool Rd (7) plus 6 Multi-views or "Compo's" as Valentines called them (these first appear in 1925). The longest sequences are 96350-4, 209541-6, 214670-4, 221270-4, 221508-12, G3643-56 & H2628-33. **2 of Blundellsands** in 1905 - Bridge Rd (47825) & Blundellsands Rd West (49236). **17 of Bootle**, 6 in 1905 (49761-6), 6 in 1914 (78536-41) plus 4 dock scenes and a Multi-view - all of predictable sites (except 49763 of the Canal). **58 of Formby & 13 of Freshfield** between 1913 & 1939 covering most of the area with half being Shore related. The longest sequences being 77138-45, 201938-43, 209803-13, G3638-42, H15-22 and 212860-3, 223990-4 with 6 Multi-views noted. **8 of Gt. Crosby** (47826-33), **4 of Ince Blundell** (49170-2 & 50183), **2 of Litherland** (49109-10), **3 of Little Crosby** (48303-4 & 49169), **6 of Lydiate** (47256-60 & 49166), **7 of Seaforth** (47967-71 & 49108 & 78754) and **1 of Thornton** (49165) - all bar one from 1905 with the majority being typical subjects but no Multi-views. **92 of Waterloo** evenly spread between 1905 & 1939 which include 6 Multi-views. Apart from 22 taken of main roads (8 are South Road), almost all the remainder are predictable Coastline subjects. The longest sequences are 47958-65, 56970-6, 91026-33, 216124-33, G5162-8 & G6740-7.

According to names in the registers, the majority were taken (or arranged) by :- the 1905 material by **H.J.S.Anderton** of Birkdale, Southport, then **J.Leigh** of Abergele (1906-7). An anonymous spell from then to 1912 is followed by Manchester-based **Wm.H.Bowman's** efforts up to 1926. He was succeeded by **J.Farmer** & **J.G.Scrutton** to beyond 1939, who almost certainly acted as photographers and agents. Not having commercial premises of their own, it would appear they were solely in the employ of the company. If certain areas seem to have had an inordinate number of views issued, remember that not all circulated at the same time - many were replaced when fashion and other factors dated them.

SHORE ROAD, AINSDALE. ·H.2629.

Selected Sefton issues including date of withdrawal (if applicable).

47827	1905	VICARAGE FARM, GREAT CROSBY - withdrawn 1938
49110	1905	RECREATION GROUND, LITHERLAND - withdrawn 1936
49763	1905	LEEDS & LIVERPOOL CANAL, BOOTLE - withdrawn 1963
78536	*1914*	*STRAND RD, BOOTLE - withdrawn 1936, see ill. opposite*
91029	1924	GENERAL HOSPITAL, WATERLOO - withdrawn 1932
201984	1927	THE OLD MILL, AINSDALE - withdrawn 1935
209791	1930	WOODVALE, AINSDALE
209812	1930	THE LIGHTHOUSE, FORMBY
212366	1931	BOOTLE CHILDREN'S HOLIDAY CAMP, FORMBY
223993	1933	PINE WOOD, FRESHFIELD
G 3647	1935	TENTLAND, AINSDALE - withdrawn 1954
H 2629	*1939*	*SHORE ROAD, AINSDALE - see illustration below left*

Note : Collectors of Valentine cards may obtain the full list of issues for this area (between 1900 - 1939) which includes the above information, district by district. <u>Send a blank uncrossed £1 Postal Order & foolscap SAE</u> to the publisher for a copy by return - cheque or non SAE orders will be destroyed.

(both) Valentine No. H 2629 of 1939 (left) showing Shore Road bus gyratory and a Southport service ex Roe Lane - the CLC Ainsdale Beach station is just visible in the distance. Although not postally used until 1954, the sender states that the recent closure of the station (1952), has fostered talk of a coastal road being built on the trackbed. Mention is also made of special beach buses.... (Above) A *Rimmer, Harrison & Sutherland* Bedford QL open bus on Southport Sands in the 50's. This seasonal Corporation service began in 1946 and operated along the shore until the mid 60's. (courtesy of R.F.Mack)

INDEX

Liverpool Road, Crosby, around 1916 showing Henderson's Confectioners & Tea Rooms at No.95 and next door at 97 which was split between the Eldon Hairdressing Saloon & Merrick's Newsagents (between Queens Road and Endbutt Lane). Being un-marked, this is likely to have been a Stephen Cushing 'commission' - with no real competitor in the immediate area at that time, this theory is supported by the card having been sent to a relative of the posed group. The abundance of postcards in their window further suggests they did business with him on a regular basis.